THE REFUTATION OF S

THE REFUTATION OF SCEPTICISM

A.C. Grayling

Duckworth

First published in 1985 by
Gerald Duckworth & Co. Ltd
The Old Piano Factory
43 Gloucester Crescent, London NW1

ISBN 0 7156 1922 5

British Library Cataloguing in Publication Data

Grayling, A.C.
The refutation of scepticism.
1. Skepticism
I. Title
121'5 BD201

ISBN 0-7156-1922-5

Photoset in North Wales by
Derek Doyle & Associates, Mold, Clwyd
Printed and bound in Great Britain by
Unwin Brothers Ltd, Old Woking

Contents

Preface vii

1. Introduction 1
2. The Naturalistic Reply to Scepticism 10
3. 'Conceptual Schemes' and Relativism 40
4. Transcendental Arguments 77

Appendices
1. Empiricism and the *a priori* 114
2. Knowledge, belief and beliefs 128
3. The justification regress and foundationalism 132
4. The forms of scepticism 138
5. Realism and perceptual discourse 140
6. A note on certainty 144

Bibliography 146
Index 149

In memory of my mother,
Ursula Grayling.

Preface

It has been a temptation lately for philosophers to give a Humean shrug when faced with the problem of our knowledge of the external world. This reaction seems to me perfectly right, and in what follows I attempt to spell out why.

This book is not a study of epistemological scepticism as such, which is a tedious and over-familiar topic. Thc varieties of sceptical argument, rehearsed and discussed in well-known works by Descartes, Russell, Ayer, Austin and others, get barely a mention here; I assume that the reader knows them. What they come down to, taken together, is the claim that since it is never a contradiction to assert the conjunction of the best evidence we have for some epistemological claim *p* with the denial of *p*, we can never be fully justified in believing what we normally take ourselves to believe about the world. The task I set myself here is to refute this claim. It seems to me that the lessons to be learned from, on the one hand, the naturalism of Hume and Wittgenstein and, on the other, the transcendentalism of Kant will show how to achieve this end. The sequel is devoted to that task.

In order to keep the outlines of the argument uncluttered I have treated certain preliminaries and longer parenthetical points as appendices. The appendices are, in effect, long footnotes.

The argument gets more tendentious as it proceeds, and is most tendentious of all in its metaphysical claims at the end, where the suggestion is, strongly, that solving our epistemological difficulties with a Humean shrug commits us to idealism, a consequence which does not dismay me. I hope to discuss these metaphysical issues in detail elsewhere.

The argument of this book grew out of work done in the course of my doctoral research at Oxford between 1976 and 1981. Accordingly I take pleasure in thanking the supervisors of that earlier work, Professors Sir Alfred Ayer and Sir Peter Strawson, for their help, and its examiners, Lord Quinton and Professor D.W. Hamlyn, for their comments, all of which pointed the way for further development.

I am grateful to successive generations of students and an enduring generation of friends for discussion of various topics associated, more or less closely, with issues raised in the following. Conversations with Timothy Sprigge, Marcus Giaquinto, David McNaughton and Michael Luntley have, in particular, provided much enjoyable and profitable philosophical stimulus, and my warm thanks go to them. I am grateful too to Susan Whitfield, who has made it possible for me to say *redditus orbis est*, which says a great deal.

While this volume was in proof there appeared books on scepticism by Stroud and by Hacker and Baker, and an Aristotelian Society debate between Lear and Stroud (*Supp. Vol.* 58 1984) entitled 'The Disappearing "We" ', all which are relevant to the argument of the sequel. These discussions reinforce my conviction that the line pursued here is the most fruitful one available to us in this important and difficult region of thought, and it is pleasing to find that the solution proposed here, and the form which its proposal takes, squarely fits the problems as they are identified by these participants in the renewed debate.

Oxford A.C.G.

CHAPTER ONE

Introduction

The aim in what follows is to refute scepticism concerning our knowledge of the external world. That is the traditional way of putting things; more accurately, the aim is to demonstrate the vacuity of sceptical doubt concerning the justification of our ordinary empirical beliefs.

Scepticism would be a boring and trivial issue indeed did it not have at least one genuinely troublesome form. The apparent vacuity of some sceptical doubts arises from the fact that they are directed against notions of knowledge, justification or rationality which, upon inspection, turn out to be artificially restrictive. Thus a sceptical argument which consists in a definition of knowledge of such a kind as to rule out anything's ever being an item of knowledge is a sceptical argument of a wholly idle kind, and this is not the sort which is of interest here.

What we are concerned to show is how we can be justified in making assertions of the general purport: this is how things stand in the world. Scepticism about our ever being satisfactorily justified in *this* enterprise is interesting, and we are likely to learn a lot by attempting to defeat it. Such scepticism consists in the conjunction of (a) a set of psychological contingencies relating to the main sources of our evidence for what we take to be the way things are in the world with (b) certain crucial questions about the nature of justification and the danger of uncontrollable justification regress. The former, (a), are the familiar considerations about perceptual relativities, illusion, error, dreaming or systematic deception by a Cartesian demon, and the latter, (b), are outlined in Appendix 3. In sum, sceptical queries arising from these sets of considerations, taken together, issue in the sceptical point that it at least appears to be the case that it is never a contradiction to state the best evidence for any assertion we care to make about the world in conjunction with the denial of that assertion, so that we appear never to be justified in making those assertions.

This can be put more explicitly by characterising the sceptical challenge like this: our possession of the best evidence for claims about the world is always consistent with the falsity of those claims – which can be summed up in the slogan '(*e*.-*p*) is not a contradiction', where *e* is the best evidence for *p*, and *p* is some claim about the world or the way something is in the world – so that we cannot regard ourselves as ever being justified in making those claims.

This is the bottom line of scepticism; it is what the familiar and well-rehearsed considerations collected as (a) and (b) above are intended to establish. It is against this that the argument of the sequel is directed.

The first stage of my argument will be that we are justified in making knowledge claims about the world on the basis of our evidence for them, for the reason that this evidence, *together with beliefs about the world which are basic to our conceptual scheme and without which we could not have coherent experience*, constitute the conditions for assertion of such knowledge claims, such that when these conditions are satisfied assertion of the relevant claims is warranted. Written into this account is the notion of a *theory of error*; particular claims that things are thus and so are defeasible, but this does not afford sceptical purchase, because in order to possess the concept of being mistaken in empirical judgments, we need to know what *counts* as being mistaken,[1] which is to say that we need to have and be able to apply a grasp of the ways such judgments go wrong and how they can be put right. The point is clearer still if the idea is characterised as one of a 'coherent discourse', or, as it might be put, a 'consistent and senseful empirical-judgment language game'. In this idiom, empirical evidence and basic beliefs, together with our implicit theory of error, jointly constitute the grounds of sense for empirical-judgment assertions. If we were not right in our judgments for the greater part of the time, and if we did not know what goes

[1] This signals a certain kind of 'paradigm case' defence, reformulated later.

wrong and how to put it right for nearly all the rest of the time, our discourse about the world would be incoherent.

Whether this way with scepticism is successful depends upon two things. First, certain controversial points need to be resolved. Among them are the notion of basic (or, as I shall give reason for calling them, 'transcendental') beliefs; the notion of a special relation between empirical evidence and transcendental beliefs, on the one hand, and empirical judgments on the other; the notion of warranted assertibility as the ground for the sense of empirical judgment talk; the notion of a 'theory of error' implicit in warrant conditions; and the notion, importantly implicit in all this, that talk of coherent experience is equivalent to talk of coherent discourse. Each of these issues will be considered at length in due course.

Secondly, if the foregoing is successfully made out, it defeats scepticism only at one level, the level of particular claims about particular matters of fact; for it says that empirical judgments are made within the context of a conceptual scheme, and their internality with respect to that scheme is what affords them their justification. The sceptic then raises his sights and challenges the notion of the scheme, and in particular the notion that its coherence depends upon transcendental beliefs somehow 'underpinning' it. What justification have we for saying that there are transcendental beliefs, that is, that there are beliefs necessary to our conceptual scheme? In advance of arriving at this point, the sceptic will question the very notion of a conceptual scheme, and attack it, if it survives, with relativist arguments; and he will assault the idea of a transcendental defence of the view that the beliefs which ultimately license knowledge claims are necessary features of our thought and talk about the world. Here again there are a number of controversial points which require careful presentation in their due place.

I shall, in the course of developing these defences against scepticism, restrict attention to transcendental arguments aimed at showing that, in order for our experience (and thus our discourse) to be coherent or intelligible, we are bound to assume that physical objects exist independently of our perception of them. If this is an assumption we cannot do without, sceptical doubts about the independent existence of physical objects are vacuous; and we will have derived at least one of the central foundational beliefs upon which the rest of our epistemic structure is erected, and by reference to which justification for particular knowledge claims can be secured. (Success in this respect will also therefore justify a foundationalist approach to epistemology: see Appendix 3). For reasons which will become clear in the working out of the transcendental arguments, their effect upon the sceptic, if successful, might best be described as defeating rather than refuting him. The distinction is a fine one, and because either one amounts to the required objective – settling sceptical doubt – it makes little difference to whether or not the enterprise here is as a whole successful. It does however make a difference to our metaphysics, for it has, as I shall show, an unexpected consequence.

The enterprise in hand, then, is to show that scepticism is to be dealt with by demonstrating how our ordinary empirical judgments are underpinned by beliefs playing a foundational role in our conceptual scheme, and that if this manoeuvre is successful, it will force the sceptic to shift his attention to the question of the scheme as a whole and its stock of basic, or, as I shall shortly give reason for calling them, transcendental beliefs. In Chapter 2 I begin upon this programme by considering the question of what role is played by transcendental beliefs and how they license our ordinary empirical judgments, thus forcing scepticism to the higher level where, in Chapters 3 and 4, his doubts about the scheme and transcendental beliefs themselves are to be met.

The reason why I call the required kind of basic beliefs 'transcendental beliefs' is twofold. First, such a usage directly echoes Kant's use of the term 'transcendental' to reflect what has to do with the conditions of possibility for experience or – which was the same thing for him – the conditions of possibility for knowledge.[2] In Kant's view 'knowledge' is the synthetic knowledge founded upon experience, and experience, in turn, is self-conscious awareness of the synthesised manifold, which as such must involve at least some knowledge.[3] The claim I seek to make is essentially similar: there are certain beliefs which are indispensable to coherent experience (*sive* coherent or intelligible discourse about the world, as will be argued), and it is therefore appropriate to characterise their

[2] *Critique of Pure Reason* B161, B218.
[3] Cf. R.C.S. Walker, *Kant*, London 1979, p. 10.

fundamental role in experience as *transcendental* in precisely the Kantian sense. Secondly, these beliefs are, in virtue of their foundational role, beliefs of the sort characterised in Appendix 3 as non-inferential and 'in some sense' self-justifying. The sense which 'self-justification' has here is revealed by the fact that the status of these beliefs is such that their place in the scheme requires demonstration by transcendental argument. Because they are transcendentally justified, therefore, it is again appropriate to characterise them as transcendental beliefs.

Some informal considerations will help to set the stage for showing how transcendental beliefs provide the basis for justification of our beliefs about the external world. They are as follows.

In ordinary circumstances, when someone claims that such and such is the case, he may be challenged to justify his claim; and he will do so by appealing to what will count for him and his interlocutors as evidence appropriate to establishing his claim. In general, there are three standard outcomes in such proceedings; either the claimant will furnish evidence which he and his interlocutors will agree settles the matter, or his interlocutors will compel him to withdraw his claim either by furnishing countervailing evidence or by showing him that his evidence does not support his claim; or there will be open disagreement concerning whether the available evidence does or does not support the claim. In the great majority of cases where agreement is reached, the chain of evidence appealed to will be short owing to the broad consensus among sharers of a conceptual scheme concerning what kind of evidence settles what kind of claim. In ordinary cases where claims are left undecided by disputants, it will not be, generally, because of profound philosophical dilemmas concerning justification, but because the evidence is insufficient, or because the disputants' grasp of it – or the motives, choices, and policies affecting their grasp of it – renders it insufficient to decide the claim. Often we are content to assign probabilities in the case of insufficient evidence, the standard means of deciding odds as to which horse will win the next race; or, as in the second variant, in cases of disputes about, for example, what strategy it is best to pursue in governing the nation, tendencies are for us to select and interpret such evidence as will best serve our prior theoretical commitments (a Quinean point).

These considerations show that *philosophical* doubt about justification for our claims is, when contrasted with everyday cases, decidedly peculiar. The sceptic is not interested in being told that if he wishes to test my claim to such and such an effect, he can go and look, or feel, or test-drive one himself; he will simply say that doing all *that* is not to the point. The problem is rather, in the case of any claim we care to make about the way things are in the world, what at bottom justifies us in believing what we are committed to in making such a claim?

Now, suppose we imagine a case in which a philosophical sceptic tries to get someone, who is accustomed to the ordinary standards for appealing to evidence, to see the point of such sceptical doubt. The sceptic may be attempting to convince the layman that there are grounds for doubt as to whether they are justified in believing that, for example, there is a table here before them. Perhaps he does so by appeal to particular sceptical considerations of the philosophically familiar sort about perceptual relativities and so forth, or perhaps he directly makes the wholly general point about the logical gap between evidence and empirical judgments which these familiar considerations are intended to display. The layman may well, in puzzled exasperation, come out with the remark: 'But if this isn't a case of seeing a table and knowing that it's there, I don't know what is!' The sceptic presses him to explain; and the layman's response contains what is philosophically crucial: instead of repeating that he sees and feels the table, which he knows leaves the sceptic unmoved, he tells a more general story, to this effect: if one is to have an orderly world-view, such that one can act, predict and communicate with the large measure of success required to pursue the most mundane of lives, it is necessary that the world be regarded as stable and regular, with at least largely orderly connections between different states of affairs, and with it being possible for us as perceivers and communicators to discriminate among items of our shared experience, to identify and reidentify such items, and on the whole to succeed both in making reference to them and in describing them. Any particular perceptual judgment is internal to this scheme, or, alternatively put, presupposes this scheme. In saying 'This is a table' we are *implicitly* claiming that here in our perceptual environment is a spatio-temporal continuant, with all that this entails, and that we have perceptual access to it; and we are *explicitly* claiming that this object is to be classified according to those everyday conventions which facilitate our sortings of objects relative to our interests. This latter proceeding would be impossible without what is presupposed, namely the scheme. In saying that we are justified in asserting that here is a table, we are therefore saying that we are committed to a realist conceptual scheme which has it that there is a plurality of spatio-temporal continuants in casual relations among themselves and with us, and that this is the root of our justification. Clearly, the sceptic's challenge is not a challenge over the question of our linguistic and classificatory conventions as such; rather, it is a challenge about the ontological presuppositions of our thought and talk (i.e., 'Are you sure there is a table here?' is not intended to convey 'Might it not be a chair?' but 'What justifies you in taking it that there is a distinct continuous existent here?'). The task in hand therefore is to make out these presuppositions clearly, and to show (which is the task of the following chapters) how they are justified. To make out these presuppositions clearly, the informal sketch just given needs to be turned into a detailed account.

Before turning to that project, however, it is useful and instructive to look at a way in which the intuitions just sketched could be presented as a philosophical account, a way which seems to me correct and in direct accordance with the views I go on to argue for, but which is insufficiently detailed and too metaphorical to serve in its own right. This way of putting matters owes itself to Hume and Wittgenstein.

It is possible and indeed fruitful to see both Hume and Wittgenstein as 'naturalists' in respect of their response to scepticism.[4] In Book I Part IV of the *Treatise* Hume gives his celebrated reasons for refusing to concede to scepticism about the existence of body and induction by stating that nature (hence the label 'naturalist') does not leave the matter of our belief in these two respects to *reason*, for reason is wholly inadequate to prove or justify those beliefs; but, rather, gives us no choice with respect to them; we simply *have* to believe thus; we *must* judge as we *must* eat and breathe; and accordingly it is vain so much as to raise the question whether or not body exists or our inductions are justified.

[4] The label and the comparison are Strawson's; they occur in his unpublished lectures given at Oxford 1977-9.

Wittgenstein did not appeal explicitly to nature in his notes *On Certainty*, but the echo is there. He distinguished between what it is profitless to speculate about in the way of our beliefs, and what it is profitable to speculate about; such beliefs as that there are physical objects fall into the first category. Such beliefs are *beyond* speculation; our commitment to them is 'animal' (§359), which recalls Hume's view that belief is more properly a function of the sensitive than the cogitative part of our nature. Such beliefs, for Wittgenstein, are 'exempt from doubt' (341), because they have a 'special role in our frame of reference' (83) as the 'substratum' (162), 'scaffolding' (211) or 'element' (105) (in the sense of air or water) of our ordinary, testable, empirical beliefs. Thus special beliefs constitute the 'foundation' (411, 415, 401) and 'underlie' (415) ordinary empirical beliefs (although Wittgenstein intended neither of these notions to be understood in a traditional foundationalist sense).

Wittgenstein, in line with his aversion to system, neither gave a list of these special beliefs, nor specified the difference between them and ordinary empirical beliefs. Indeed, it is not clear that all the special beliefs are, as it were, forever special; for in the river analogy (96-9) where ordinary beliefs are likened to the flowing water, and special beliefs to the river-bed and banks, Wittgenstein remarks that the bed and banks consist both of hard rock and sand, which latter is, in the process of time, eroded away. However, the hard rock does not shift (cf. his saying of special beliefs that they are 'fast' and 'solid' at 151).

The presentation Wittgenstein gave of this position is highly metaphorical; but there are one or two firmer considerations, and they are of great value. He characteristically likened special beliefs to *rules*, and said that in an important sense propositions like 'physical objects exist' are nonsense (36), or cannot be formulated (34), owing to the special role the belief in the existence of objects plays in our thought, talk and action (at 342 the indubitability of beliefs like this one is characterised as: indubitability in *practice*, in *act*, in *fact*). Questions of doubt and knowledge accordingly arise only in connection with ordinary empirical beliefs.[5]

The view being urged in these similar ways by Hume and

[5] The extensive debate on Wittgenstein's notion of rules and rule-following cannot be investigated here, but I think it by no means irrelevant to some of the argument below.

Wittgenstein is that sceptical doubts are wholly idle, and there is no point either in asserting or denying them; scepticism is not an option. With this view – and, indeed, for the reasons given by Hume and Wittgenstein in its support – I wholly concur. However, neither goes far enough or attempts to pin down in any detail the way the highly general and fundamental beliefs in question operate in our thought and talk. It may in fact be that, at certain points, metaphor *is* our only resource in this region of thought – metaphor sometimes functions as a kind of showing rather than saying and might be taken to have maieutic status. But it is incumbent upon us at least to try to be more specific about the role of the special beliefs, and about how scepticism is to be recognised as idle in the light of them, than either Hume or Wittgenstein were; and to this attempt I now turn.

The argument proceeds as follows: in Chapter 2 I show how the sense of perceptual judgment talk and the coherence of the experience reported by such talk demand the same 'transcendental beliefs' as necessary conditions; in Chapter 3 I defend the notion of a conceptual scheme and argue that there is only one scheme; and in Chapter 4 I discuss transcendental arguments themselves and defend them against criticisms.[6]

[6] Appendices 1-4 below contain discussions of points which are, effectively, preliminaries to what follows but not an integral part of the argument. Appendix 1 shows that the argument here does not mark a break with the broadly empiricist tradition of modern philosophy; Appendices 2 and 3 deal with two matters of an important but incidental nature concerning the notions of belief and justification respectively; and Appendix 4 is a note on the forms that sceptical argument can take.

CHAPTER TWO

The Naturalistic Reply to Scepticism

The first stage of the argument is to show that ordinary empirical judgments are secure from sceptical challenge on the ground that they are internal to a scheme which provides them with their justification. This is the task in the present chapter. Success here will mean that the sceptic has to tackle the notion of the justifying scheme itself, and the beliefs basic to it; this higher-level scepticism is dealt with in the later chapters.

Giving a detailed account of what transcendental beliefs are, and how they underlie our thought and talk of the world, involves a number of steps. I wish to begin by distinguishing between three classes of beliefs. This classification is broad and not exhaustive, and it is intended merely as a working classification for the purposes in hand.

First, there is the class of transcendental beliefs which I shall argue are necessarily presupposed to our thought and talk of the world in general. Secondly there is what I shall call a class of 'perceptual beliefs', beliefs about states of affairs in one's perceptual environment. Central members of this class are the beliefs expressed by such statements, which I shall call 'perceptual statements', as 'This is a table', 'Her dress is red', 'There are two birds on the branch', and so on, that is, statements about the way things are in perceptual heres and nows. I shall be most concerned with these two classes of beliefs.

The third class of beliefs I shall loosely designate 'general beliefs'. Although I shall not be concerned with these to any great extent, they present a number of problems, some of which I shall for more general reasons be dealing with in the next chapter. The following brief account of them will suffice to indicate the role they play.

General beliefs are typified by 'Deciduous trees lose their leaves in autumn', 'Most people have two eyes', 'Water can extinguish fire' and so on, that is, general hypotheses about the properties and behaviour of kinds of things in the world, or the way common occurences usually turn out. General beliefs constitute the broad theory about how things are and work, and range from attested scientific theories to common-sense rules of thumb. They are on the whole probabilistic, which is to say that they are open to revision under pressure of new data. On such a view, scientific theories are to be interpreted instrumentally, not as uncovering what there is in some ultimate sense, but as constituting best explanations relative to the data so far available. I do not wish to argue for some such strong claim as that theory is always historically parochial *and* that this entails the falsity of views about convergence; for it is not implausible to hold that if we are bound by the terms of a conceptual scheme to have a certain broadly determinate phenomenology of experience, there may well be a limit to the best model we can construct to explain the objects of that experience. Thus, if it were true that the coherence and intelligibility of our conceptual scheme rests upon our being committed to assuming that there are physical objects, then there may be no better means of explanation and prediction regarding such objects than by working with the model that they are (as if) comprised of charged particles and so on. This would remain true even if idealism were true. I am not of course claiming that scientific theory is *no more* than that; only that the truth of convergence can be maintained without its being the case that the terminus of convergence is the truth about the world (as for instance was argued by Peirce), but, instead, that its terminus is the best possible model of the objects we take ourselves to experience. This way with the matter of convergence provides the basis of an account in which it can be squared with idealism; which I remark, not to defend such an account here, but for two independent reasons. One is to show that general beliefs, including current scientific theories, do not of themselves provide a way of refuting scepticism, for they are not at all the right kind of beliefs to serve at the foundation of our conceptual scheme, but are, as it were, epistemologically super-structural rather than foundational. An alternative way of putting this is to say that any theory about the world generalised from the way the world appears to us in our experience of it, has to 'save' that appearing; what the theory has in the end to explain is the collection of items which we take ourselves to see and hear. The second reason is that it shows that any view which does not issue in an acceptance of the standard view about the consequences of convergence does not *ipso facto* entail relativism. One cannot argue that there are transcendental beliefs necessary to our conceptual scheme and at the same time allow conceptual relativism. (Cultural relativism, which is different, presents no difficulty.) This matter will be dealt with more fully in due course.

General beliefs have as their major function the filling–out of the world–story to which we as percipients have fragmentary and local access. Objects and events partially and discontinuously perceived from a person's limited local point of view are fleshed out, and connected with the rest of the world and history (or at any rate sizeable portions of both) by general beliefs. By means of these beliefs we can have particular expectations, make particular predictions and pursue policies. In short, general beliefs constitute our world-picture in much the sense characterised aptly (although I borrow) by Strawson as 'the web ... of our historical and geographical knowledge in general'.[1]

General beliefs have a great deal to do with the epistemic valuations we place upon perceptual beliefs. If someone rushed out of a church saying that he had just seen an angel, the response of his audience would be determined by the general beliefs currently held by them. In A.D. 1400 someone's claiming such an experience might well have been taken as evidence for an act of special providence by God; six centuries later it might instead be taken as evidence for hysteria, dementia, disingenuousness or just gross credulity on the claimant's part. The dependence of the truth-value of assertions in general upon the general beliefs constituting at least part of the verifying or falsifying background to them, together with the nature of general beliefs themselves, makes the analysis of statements about the world rather more complex a matter than one might wish it to be. 'You were born of woman' said to any human being is currently taken to be (on Kripkean lines) a necessary truth, but will cease to be

[1] Strawson, 'Identifying reference and truth-values' in *Logico-Linguist Papers*, 1971, p. 77; and see especially his *The Bounds of Sense*, London 1966, pp. 143-5.

one in due process of developments in medical technology; at that future time it may on any occasion of utterance be true, but no longer because it is necessary. (This is surely a problem for Kripkeans.) One could say that at present such an assertion is a statement of policy but in time will be a defeasible statement of fact. For any number of assertions about the way things are in the world, then, the warrant one has for making them is contingent upon theory which is at least in principle defeasible. For anyone committed to an antirealist view of truth, to the effect that truth is not verification-transcendent, such a reflection supports his view. This would appear to be another reason to think relativism true; but again, it is not. Any general belief has, as remarked, to 'save the appearances'. The appearances may well be theory-soaked, in the sense that the classificatory conventions governing our sortings of objects,[2] and the means by which we describe them, may indeed be relative to our theories about objects – but *that* they are objects is an issue presupposed to our being able to classify them as objects *of certain kinds*. This is to say that transcendental beliefs, that is, beliefs to the effect that there are spatio-temporal, causally-interactive items existing independently of our perception of them, are presupposed to there being any theory about the perceived world at all; transcendental beliefs do not constitute a theory about the world in anything like the sense at issue, but are conditions of there being such theories. If transcendental beliefs are necessary to experience, then there are constraints upon the number of competing theories there can be in order to explain and classify the objects in whose existence we are thus committed to believing. Moreover, since the different competing theories range over the same objects, these theories will be (in a sense to be explained when relativism is discussed more fully later) mutually accessible. Both these considerations check the inclination to take it, as a consequence of the nature of general beliefs and the role they play in particular

[2] I use 'object' here and throughout, unless qualified, to mean those items in our experience which we take to be spatio-temporal continuants existing independently of our perception of them. This is the 'full-blooded' concept of objects in Strawson's sense, *Bounds of Sense*, p. 16. I shall use the term, in addition, to include 'States of Affairs' which are comprised of such objects and the events in which they are involved. Thus for 'objects' read 'perception-independent spatio-temporal continuants, and states of affairs composed of or involving them'.

judgments about the world, that relativism is true.

These comments on general beliefs are too brief, but they will have to suffice. The issues of truth, relativism and a respectable characterisation of the notion of a 'conceptual scheme' will re-emerge and be discussed in due course. It is enough to say at this juncture that the claim is that transcendental beliefs are presupposed to general beliefs in much the same way as they are presupposed to the making of particular perceptual judgments; and this latter is the claim I am concerned to argue for now.

Perception is the source and test of contingent knowledge. This is a principle to which I shall be bound here, and I shall argue that it is by showing how we understand perception and perceptual talk that we can show how the justification of our beliefs, as demanded by the sceptic, can be secured. So much is in any case obvious.

It is sometimes thought to be appropriate to characterise perception as a marriage of intuition (in Kant's sense) and intellection (that is, the application of concepts), for the two reasons that, first, to perceive something is always to perceive it as something of a certain kind, and secondly, that no case of sensory experience can be 'raw' in Feigl's sense of 'raw feels', because we should deny that mere sensory stimulation (even if it evokes response, as in the case of the reflex jerk in the legs of decerebrate frogs whose feet are electrically stimulated) amounts to experience, unless certain further conditions are satisfied; which is the force of Kant's holding that experience consists in self-conscious awareness (*CPR* B161), a condition of which is that concepts be applied to the manifold of intuition so that it can be presented by the percipient to himself as an array of objects, experience of which he recognises as his own.

However, although in a way it is informative to make a distinction between intuition *simpliciter* and perception as conceptualised intuition, it is also misleading; for it suggests intuition can be characterised independently of perception, that is that the contents of our sensory states can be characterised by means of a 'purely sensory vocabulary' which carries no reference to objects of perception. This is explicitly argued for by Ayer.[3] But it is impossible, for the following reasons.

In describing the contents of our sensory states, we have to utilise

[3] Cf. Ayer's views as characterised below in Appendix 5.

predicables of quality like 'red', 'round', 'striped', 'blurred' and the like. The literal and primary use of such predicables is to describe and sort objects; balls are red and round, zebras are striped, edges of pictures blurred. The best we can do in attempting to prise apart what is 'directly present' to us in our sensory states and the objects which we normally suppose to bear such qualities is to retreat from perceptual statements; this is a point made by Austin and Strawson. Thus we can prefix 'It is as if I were seeing/feeling ...' to an ordinary perceptual statement, as a way of effecting the 'progressive hedging' of which Austin talks, or Strawson's 'step back' from perceptual statements.[4] But this shows that the predicables used to characterise the contents of our sensory states are being used in a metaphorical sense, one derivative upon their standard application, and cannot therefore be used to describe the contents of our sensory states independently of what, by the standard use of the perceptual statements retreated from, we are normally committed to believing exists. Certainly it would not do to reify the contents of sensory states and hold that *they* can be red, round and so on; postulating a further array of existents between percipients and objects is worse than philosophically redundant; it exacerbates rather than solves difficulties about perception, which is shown by the sense-data debate in some of its variants. It is of no use, therefore, to hold that there are two kinds of items which can be red and round, namely objects and sense-data; and this is not just because it is merely *natural* to describe our experience by talking about the objects it is experience of, but because *there is no other way of doing so*. For cases of hallucination or dreaming we grasp that they *are* such cases exactly by saying that they are cases in which the objects of the experience enjoyed were indeed absent; we say we 'seemed' to see such and such, or it 'appeared as if' such and such, but it was not in fact such and such. This is just what specifies them as cases of that kind.[5] Now, to argue that one's sensory states cannot be described except by means of terms whose literal function is to describe objects is to say that description of experience carries *essential reference* to its actual or possible objects; which is to say that there is no possible

[4] See Appendix 5 for an important expansion of the discussion here.
[5] Identifying such cases is a matter of taking into account a longer and fuller story, along the lines of Descartes' suggestion in *Meditations* VI.

characterisation of experience which is made without essential use of the concepts and terms by means of which the objects of experience are described. The vocabulary used to talk about objects just is the vocabulary we use to talk about experience; there are not two vocabularies, nor does the one vocabulary have, as it were, two readings. There are various ways of driving the point home; for example, we can ask whether there can be an intuition-language (a purely phenomenal language) whose construction is in no way parasitic upon, derived from, or uniformly correspondent to, an object-language, given that the items picked out by the former – rednesses, shrillnesses, roughnesses, tartnesses – would all of them match (and would have to match, if the intuition-language is to be used to explain perception) the qualities of objects by means of which, in our pre-philosophical innocence, we identify and sort those objects. Clearly we *could* duplicate quality expressions by inventing words or a code, but to what purpose? In virtue of their matchings to the expressions we already have, the same reference to objects of experience would carry through.

The readiest way to view this issue is in the light of the standard empiricist claim concerning the relation between experience and knowledge of objects, namely that the former is the source or foundation of the latter. Familiarly, for anyone concerned to show how experience can give rise to knowledge of an external world, it appears right and natural to investigate *experience* itself, if possible shrived of its ontological commitments, in order to see how far it will bear the realist view which pre-theoretically we load upon it. This is the approach that was taken at one time by Ayer (See Appendix 5). Phenomenalism is a direct consequence of it, for when we find that experience does not underwrite inferences to objects (in the full-blooded sense of independent reals) an analysis has to be given which will show how, none the less, experience and the world are related. The phenomenalist suggestion is that talk of objects is equivalent to talk of sense experiences and that, as a corollary of the fact that the former are to be analysed into the latter, objects are to be regarded as constructions out of sense-data (that is, the contents, in some meaning of the term, of sense experiences).

This standard and familiar phenomenalist view is readily opposed by the equally standard objections to the notion of sense-data. For present purposes this dispute is neither here nor there; what is crucial is that phenomenalist and cognate views issue in the claim that it is upon sense experience that our beliefs about the world are based, or from which they are constructed, and that therefore sense experience is ontologically prior to what we believe is in the world. These points are sustainable only if the starting-point for them is valid, namely the assumption that experience can be investigated in abstraction from its ontological commitments, or, as Ayer put it, the assumption that a 'purely sensory vocabulary' can be constructed to receive reductive translations from ordinary talk.

The objection to the idea that sense experiences have ontological priority to their objects is urged by Strawson in an earlier source (see Appendix 5). The phenomenalist claim that sense experiences are prior can only be made if they are identifiable and discussable independently of their objects; but how could we identify them without making reference to their objects? Because, therefore, descriptions of sense experiences carry such reference, it is circular and hence trivial to claim that statements about experience are equivalent to statements about objects. The circularity vitiates the theory. It would not do for a defender of the kind of phenomenalist line here in question to argue, in response, that although identifying experiences trades upon identifying objects, objects are none the less only *mentioned* and not *referred to*; for claiming to know what one's own experience consists in *does* involve reference to objects, which can be seen from the fact that to describe one's experiences is to answer the question 'What is the experience like'? whether asked by oneself or another – and such an answer can only be given if the answerer is committed to belief in the existence of publicly accessible states of affairs in terms of which saying what the experience is like can be understood.

By the same token, since there is no characterisation of experience which does not utilise the concepts of the things and their properties which we pre-theoretically take that experience to be of, neither are there concepts whose application is 'valid' or 'legitimate', in Kant's sense, without their applications being governed by experience, or, to use the terms of the misleading model repudiated above, which are not concepts which conceptualise actual or possible intuitions. This is the force of what Strawson calls Kant's 'principle of significance' (*Bounds of Sense*, p. 16). Any concept which does any work for us is one which we can find applied in particular experience-situations or situations allied to them,[6] or which in terms of our general beliefs as a whole we could rationally expect to find applicable in some such situation. Thus the distinction between, for example, concepts of psi-particles and concepts of entelechies. The notion of testing or verifying a perceptual statement is just the notion of seeing whether the concepts stated to apply in a given case *do* apply. The test of 'going and looking', accepted in all everyday cases for testing challenged visual claims, is a test of whether or not there is such and such an object with such and such properties; and so, *mutatis mutandis*, for perceptions in general.

Arguing that experience can be characterised only by the use of concepts of objects and their properties, and that such concepts are 'valid' or 'legitimate' only when there are experience-situations, or situations related to these, in which they can be applied, provides the first stage of the argument to the conclusion that I am after here, namely that perceptual judgments, which report that subclass of experiences in which we take ourselves to be justified in believing that there are objects, necessarily presuppose transcendental beliefs. The nature of the intimate and reciprocal link between experience and its objects[7] (which, as I shortly argue, is the same thing as description of experience and description of its objects) as just characterised brings with it the notion (a slightly weaker one than I require, but a step in the right direction) that our thought and talk is always and essentially conducted in terms of concepts of objects and their properties – which is to say, that our thought and talk is permeated by realist presumptions. What needs to be shown is that certain of the concepts essentially invoked in *characterising* experience are *necessary to having* that experience. It is the work of a transcendental argument to effect this, and we are still some way from being in a position to effect one; there are a number of further issues to be settled first.

In the preceding paragraph it was remarked that perceptual

[6] The rider is added to show that, for instance, concepts of colours not in the visible range of the spectrum are none the less governed by conditions of application which are either empirical or are allied to such.

[7] This is shorthand for 'experience and the objects which we take the experience to be *of*'; that is to say, 'objects' does not serve here as a generic title for the intentional accusatives of experience, but has the sense given above in note 2.

judgments report a subclass of experiences, namely that in which we take ourselves to be justified in believing that in, or by means of, those experiences we have access to objects. The force of this is to allow that there are experiences in having which we are not justified in believing that we are presented with objects; for we make mistakes, hallucinate and dream. The sceptical arguments are not mere fabrications. Our being able to discriminate among experiences in this way has of course been one of the motives for attempts, like Ayer's, to insist on our being able to characterise experience in a way which carries no commitment to the existence of objects. But there is a confusion here. Ayer and others required a characterisation of experience which is ontologically non-committal and believed that this had to be done by using something like a 'purely sensory vocabulary', as we have seen. Whereas the latter is not possible, the former is; but, informatively for our purposes, it cannot be done by shriving talk of experience of its objectivity concepts.

The means is furnished by a suggestion of Hinton's.[8] This is that the content of sensory states is to be described by means of an exclusive disjunction, one of the disjuncts of which is a perceptual judgment. Regardless of whether I know what sensory state I am in – that is, of whether I am indeed perceiving *x* or merely hallucinating or dreaming that I see *x* – I can none the less capture the sense of how it is with me sensorily, without committing myself to the existence, in that case, of the sensing's objects, by saying 'Either I see *x*, or visually hallucinate *x*, or dream ...', and *mutatis mutandis* for the other sensory modalities. Because a disjunctive sensory-content statement contains a perceptual statement as one of its disjuncts, it cannot without circularity be used to analyse perceptual statements. The move is not therefore from statements describing sensory experience to statements about objects – which cannot be done because concepts of the latter are essentially involved in descriptions of the former – but from a disjunctive sensory experience statement to one of its disjuncts. The epistemic valuations we place upon the disjuncts – deciding, that is, which one's truth makes the disjunction true – depends in part upon what might be called the epistemic context; the other experiences we have, and the way they fit together, tell us whether we are perceiving an orderly fragment of an orderly world of

[8] J.M. Hinton, *Experiences*, Oxford 1973; cf. §§IIb & IIc (pp. 60-114).

objects, or whether this is one of those rarer cases of aberration, error or the like.[9] More fully, it depends on the conditions of sense for perceptual talk; an 'epistemic context' notion is part of *this* more general matter, and in giving an account of the conditions of sense for perceptual talk we would, in addition, expect to find the essential connections between descriptions of experience and descriptions of its objects at work. To questions of sense, therefore, we must now turn.

To give the 'conditions of sense for perceptual talk' might appear to be an odd enterprise, since it consists in giving just part of a theory of meaning for part of a language. To give a theory of meaning for a language is to explain sense, reference, force and point, and the way they determine each other or interact. This is an undertaking of great complexity. The right approach has been forcefully argued, by Dummett and others, to be to give an account of meaning in terms of what it is to *understand* a language. In attempting now to specify minimal conditions of *sense* for perceptual statements I shall be guided chiefly by the notion that such conditions, in line with considerations about understanding, should specify when perceptual statements are usable or assertible, when particular instances of their use are warranted, and when a warranted use of such a statement is undefeated. My use of the term 'warrant' is a restricted one; I intend it to refer to the evidential backing available on a particular perceptual occasion for a perceptual statement; when the warrant available has the force of settling that what the perceptual statement asserts to be the case *is* the case, the warrant will be 'undefeated'. Thus 'warrant' is to be construed here as *prima facie* justification or reasonableness, and as such is defeasible; it has to do with the evidence, of any degree of strength from *prima facie* convincingness upwards, on the basis of which we make perceptual judgments.

Only a minimal characterisation is needed here. When the conditions under which a perceptual statement is assertible are specified, we need say no more in the direction of giving an account of what it is to 'understand the meaning' of the sentence used to make that statement; when the conditions under which an assertible perceptual statement is actually and non-idly asserted are such that

[9] Cf. A. Hobbs, 'New phenomenalism as an account of perceptual knowledge' in G. Vesey (ed.), *Impressions of Empiricism*, London 1976, pp. 112-15.

its assertion is warranted, we have gone most of the way to showing how our use of perceptual talk is governed by experience; and when the 'theory of error' implicit in our perceptual talk is set out we have gone as far as we need to in place of showing what it is to allocate 'truth-value' to such statements. Specification of the relevant conditions does not amount to giving the meaning or settling truth; but in any case all that is required for present purposes is that we know under what conditions perceptual statements are assertible and when non-idle assertions of them are warranted and undefeated. Specifying these conditions gives us as much of a grasp on the *sense* of perceptual statements as we need for present purposes.

A perceptual statement is one that asserts that matters are thus and such in the perceiver's present perceptual environment, that is, that there is an object in a certain location *vis-à-vis* the perceiver having certain properties (which include standing in certain relations to other objects) and/or being involved in certain objective events (that is, temporal sequences of occurrences involving objects), and so for plural cases; or it asserts that matters are thus and such with an object, event or collection of objects and events related to the perceiver's present perceptual environment. When perceptual terms, that is, the non-syncategorematic terms employed in a sentence used to make perceptual statements, are such that according to a rule they refer to or describe possible features in perceptual environments which a perceiver is able to recognise, and when these terms are grammatically concatenated, the resulting statement is one which, given the relevant circumstances, can be asserted. The 'relevant circumstances' are those in which the features referred to or described by terms in the sentence are taken by the perceiver to be present. I return to this crucial point shortly. When the perceiver, on reasonable grounds, takes such features to be present, actual and non-idle use of the sentence to make the relevant perceptual statement is warranted. Assertibility is thus the general condition of sense: grammatically concatenated terms that refer or describe, according to a rule, possible features in perceptual circumstances constitute sentences which can be used to make perceptual statements. If a term is not correlated to a possible perceptual feature (that is, if the concept expressed by the term has no empirical application within the world-picture of our general beliefs), any sentence essentially involving the term cannot be used to make a senseful perceptual statement; which is to say, no actual and non-idle use of such a perceptual statement can be warranted. Warrant thus plays this role in the general condition for sense (and in doing so therefore counts as part of the assertibility condition itself): a perceptual statement is assertible if and only if there is a possible set of circumstances in which its assertion would be warranted.

Exceptions have to be made to this characterisation of sense for perceptual statements. There are perfectly *meaningful* sentences, such as 'This is the warp-drive engine, Captain Kirk', which are not *senseful perceptual statements* according to the foregoing characterisation. It can however be allowed that fictional or imaginative objects like 'warp-drive engines' or 'Klingons' can be invoked as referents for terms in fictional or imaginative contexts, as it were by courtesy; *strictly*, however, statements essentially involving such terms are 'nonsensical' *qua* perceptual statements.

Because it is made a condition of sense for perceptual statements here that perceptual terms ('table', 'rock', 'red', 'round', that is, terms denoting or describing the objects and properties we perceive) must according to a rule refer, it might be suspected that what is covertly at work here is a denotative theory of meaning. This is not so for various reasons, although what is right about a denotative theory is, I think, captured by this view. A denotative theory of meaning for a language has it that the meanings of words are the objects they denote. This is, familiarly, a too simple and implausible view which comes nowhere near touching the complexities. The view I have just expressed regarding perceptual statements is not, however, a theory of meaning for a language, it is a specification of minimum conditions on sense for a fragment of language. Because the fragment of language in question is what we use to talk about the objects and events we take ourselves to encounter in ordinary perceptual circumstances, it is not implausible to regard a major part of the 'meaning' of perceptual statements as consisting in the fact that their constituent terms are systematically correlated by a rule to their referents. Here I leave the vexed issue of reference aside; perhaps at least some reference must be fixed by ostension; descriptions may provide referential routes for some or all non-ostensively-determined referring perceptual terms; and part of the story about some or all such reference may involve the notion of their being effected by causal or 'historical-explanation' chains, suitably construed. That perceptual statements are assertible only if the terms occuring in them can refer to (or be systematically correlated with) items in our experience says in one mode what in another mode could be put as: a perceptual statement is one in which perceptual concepts are employed, and therefore is senseful only if those concepts have possible application in our experience. This leaves it open to us to allow that 'Klingons have pointed ears' is meaningful, but is not a statement which, when actually and non-idly asserted outside the context of a 'Star-Trek' script, makes sense *qua* statement about the world.

Warrant, on the foregoing account, is not truth, and this is as it should be. It is sometimes taken to be some sort of substitute for truth, but that is a mistake; warrant is something a perceiver has for judging, on the best available evidence, that such and such is the case; 'truth' is what is taken to attach to the statement he makes if he is right. Consider for example the case where in the dark I mistakenly take a bush to be, say, a man. On the basis of the evidence, I am warranted *in judging that it is a man*, although I am not undefeatedly warranted in judging *that it is a man*. There are cases in which we are warranted by the evidence in judging that such and such is the case, only to find that such and such is not the case because of incorrect interpretation of the evidence. In any given case, however, the evidence we have, and the skill we can bring to bear upon interpreting it on that occasion, is all we have; we cannot forever reserve judgment, but must proceed according to our best lights. (This of course applies only in the *perceptual* case. In the moral case the finitary predicament can be disastrous. 'All the evidence pointed to A, but in fact it was B all along'; until *further* evidence came along, we may have been warranted in judging that A was the murderer, and, indeed, A may have hanged for it.) (This suggests, on grounds Mill would have approved, an argument against hanging). What makes for what we ordinarily think of as 'truth' ('getting it right') is warrant plus something else; at least part of the something else is a 'theory of error'.

In any particular perceptual situation I may be warranted by the available evidence in asserting an assertible perceptual statement, and be wrong. The point urged by Ryle,[10] to the effect that we grasp

[10] G. Ryle, *Dilemmas*, Cambridge 1954, pp. 94ff.

what it is to be right and to be wrong by being able to identify cases where we are right or wrong, becomes useful here. In the example just given, I discover by checking further that what I perceived was not a man but a bush. If I had been right in the first instance, there would have been further warranted perceptual judgments about a man which I could have made, forming a set with the overall characteristic that to doubt that it *is* a man I am perceptually dealing with would infect the grounds of sense for perceptual talk *tout court*; which is to say, if the set of warranted judgments I can make excludes grounds for doubt, then to continue to doubt that I am perceptually dealing with a man is worse than eccentric, it amounts to saying that the terms I employ (the concepts I apply) do not, or no longer, apply to just these perceptual situations. But if the rules connecting the employment of such terms to situations of their employment are abrogated by such doubt, then I am not and cannot be thinking or talking sensefully about this or any perceptual situation. Being wrong in making my perceptual judgment that this is a man is a case where one or more of a countably finite number of features can be found which prevent the set of my warranted judgments having the overall characteristic of *settling* that it *is* a man. In the example, closer inspection shows that I am no longer warranted in judging that it is a man; I know how and why I have gone wrong, and I have put myself right. The 'theory of error' at work in this is that in order to grasp what it is to be wrong in making a perceptual judgment, I must in general know what kinds of mistakes, or what kinds of situation, there can be in which the evidence warranting a judgment is not complete or not good enough for the judgment to count as acceptable in the light of fuller evidence. If I am warranted in making a judgment in some perceptual situation where there are no *prima facie* reasons for thinking that there is evidence against the correctness of the judgment, then I rest content with the judgment; it is, customarily, only where some grounds for doubt exist that one checks further, and what one checks for are just those features which our implicit theory of error tells us could be, and occasionally are, defeaters of our judgments.

Thus in any perceptual situation a perceptual statement I assert in connection with it is assertible, warranted and undefeated if and only if (a) the perceptual terms grammatically concatenated in the statement are correlated by a rule to the items I take myself to be perceiving in that situation, (b) the situation is such that I am able to recognise as being present the items with which the terms are so correlated, and (c) the statement together with others I do or could assert has, with these, the overall characteristic of being indubitable, in the sense that there are and can be no relevant further checks to be made, because this is the kind of situation in which (as with the layman who earlier said 'If this is not a case of seeing a table I don't know what is!') our talk about perceptual situations gets its sense. Condition (c) might better be formulated in terms of one's having to know what can go wrong with (a) or (b); put thus, (c) with (a) and (b) are severally necessary and jointly sufficient for successful standard use of perceptual statement-making sentences, knowing which is essential to having mastery of such sentences and thus a portion at least – *that* portion – of the language.

Two matters need to be commented on here. The first is that the notion of 'indubitability' I am employing is evidently stronger than some such notion as 'being beyond reasonable doubt' as characterised, for example, by Quinton, and yet does not have the force he identifies as attaching to 'incorrigible' (see Appendix 6). The second matter is that the tendency of this account of the sense-conditions for perceptual talk is strongly antirealist, and it is important to note, particularly in the light of some of my later manoeuvres, how this account accords with a general antirealist approach to meaning. It happens that both these matters can be dealt with together, as follows.

I take it that realism with respect to the fragment of language I am concerned with, namely perceptual statements, is the thesis that there are facts of the matter in virtue of which assertions are determinately true or false, and that understanding a sentence, that is, grasping the sense of a sentence, consists in knowing its truth-conditions. The truth-conditions of sentences in this fragment of language are, on the realist view, to be construed as objective states of affairs in the external world, that is, as what is the case independently of our knowledge and experience. The realist's model is the way the senses of the constants are fixed in standard logic; realism generalises from the nature of sense-fixing procedures here to a method for specifying the sense of every sentence in a language. This provides a useful way of contrasting antirealism with realism, for, as is by now well known, Dummett's opposition to realism is to a large extent inspired by intuitionism in logic and mathematics.[11] Fixing the sense of the constants in intuitionistic logic involves specifying when expressions involving them are assertible: *p.q* is assertible if and only if *p* is assertible and *q* is assertible; *pvq* is assertible if and only if at least one of them is assertible; and so on. Strictly speaking, the notion of assertibility arises from what, in intuitionist mathematical contexts, is talked of as 'effective constructability'; what is crucial in the case of language is the derived idea that grasping the sense of sentences consists in knowing a procedure for settling when one is or is not warranted in their use. What marks the advance of this form of verificationism over cruder varieties is that it does not rule out as senseless any sentence which cannot be verified or falsified as such; all that is required for a sentence to have sense is that (subject to the qualifications sketched above) there be possible warranting circumstances available for the assertion of the sentence, knowledge of which by a user of the language constitutes his grasp or understanding of the language.

There are powerful reasons for preferring the antirealist to the realist account in this connection. For one thing, as Dummett points out (§II, esp. pp. 81ff.), it is from the outset wholly obscure how connecting an assertion with a verification-transcendent truth-condition explains what it is to grasp the sense of the assertion, when *ex hypothesi* the truth-condition may or may not obtain without our being able to recognise the fact. Many of the sentences in a natural language are not effectively decidable; some examples are sentences quantified over infinite or unsurveyable domains, and counterfactuals (p. 81). For any undecidable sentence 'we cannot equate a capacity to recognise the satisfaction or non-satisfaction of the condition for the sentence to be true with a knowledge of what that condition is ... because, by hypothesis, either the condition is one which may obtain in some cases in which we are incapable of recognising the fact, or it is one which may fail to obtain in some cases in which we are incapable of recognising the fact, or both; hence a knowledge of what it is for that condition to hold or not to hold, while it may demand an ability to recognise one or other state of affairs whenever we are in a position to do so, cannot be

[11] Cf. e.g. M.A.E. Dummett, 'What is a theory of meaning? II' in Evans & McDowell (edd.), *Truth and Meaning*, Oxford 1976.

exhaustively explained in terms of that ability' (pp. 81-2). Thus Dummett's chief objection to a truth-conditional approach: 'the difficulty about a theory of meaning based on the notion of truth ... arises from the fact that the truth of many sentences of the language appear to transcend our powers of recognition' (p. 88). By contrast, a verification approach such as the one I am urging here ties grasp of the sense of sentences to the ability to recognise when it is correct to use them; someone who understands the language *displays* the fact that he does so by using the sentences on occasions when he is warranted in their use. It is because mastery of the language is displayable in this way that we are able to do what we must do in order to give an account of language understanding, namely impute to the language-user (implicit) knowledge of the sense-conditions of the language.[12] In sharp contrast, 'knowing the truth-conditions' for a sentence is not anything anyone *does* (pp. 82-3), and so it does not furnish us with means for saying what it is for someone to understand the language; and being able to say this is fundamental to giving an account of meaning.[13]

For another thing, realism leads to scepticism. On a realist view, there are two standard forms of inference, deduction and induction, available for transitions from the evidence *e* we have for any *p*, to *p*. In the case of claims about the way things are in the world, it is clear that what *e* we have for any *p* will not *entail p*; and therefore *e* and *p* are contingently related only. But this is precisely the point of departure for the sceptic; if the evidential relation of *e* to *p* is contingent, what exactly is it for *e* to be evidence for *p*? The need for an account of justification, for a theory explaining what *e* consists in and why, if at all, it entitles us to show on the basis of it how any *p* can be justifiably believed, becomes pressing. Owing to the fact that *e* and *p* are contingently related only, the sceptic's point that we can have the very best *e* for *p*, and that *p* can yet fail to be the case, is valid. Earlier I noted that the sceptic's point can be put by saying that '(*e*.–*p*) is not a contradiction', that is, that the conjunction of best *e* and *p* with the denial of *p* is not contradictory. The notion of contradiction at work here is crucial; for the realist, whatever is free from contradiction is logically possible. This provides a powerful

[12] Cf. *supra* and Dummett, ibid., pp. 70-1.

[13] M.A.E. Dummett, 'What is a theory of meaning? I' in S. Guttenplan (ed.), *Mind and Language*, Oxford 1975, p. 99.

handle to the sceptic; it does not involve a contradiction to say that I may now be dreaming, or deceived by a *malin genie*, and so forth, and so it is logically possible that I am dreaming or deceived, and thus the sceptic is able to set up the kinds of arguments intended to display the justification-gap between *e* and *p*. But on the antirealist approach, this manoeuvre is denied the sceptic because this construal of logical possibility is rejected; 'it is logically possible that *p*' in antirealist terms says in one mode what in another is put as '*p* has sense', and *p* has sense only if it can be warrantedly asserted. What could justify or warrant some such assertion as that I am deceived by a *malin genie*, that I am always at risk of perceptual error, that in *these* circumstances I may be dreaming, and so on?[14]

These last remarks explain the sense of 'indubitable' above. The evidence we have for perceptual claims stands to these latter in a meaning connection, as constituting the assertibility-condition for them. These conditions, together with the theory of error implicit in them, provide a verification procedure for perceptual statements. Error itself is, as one might put it, possible only within the limits of sense for the discourse; the boundary of error is the boundary of sense. If we have discounted error, remedied it, or (as is usually the case) have had no reason for suspecting it in connection with some *p* where *p* is a perceptual claim, then *p* is indubitable in the sense that to deny or even just doubt it is to refuse to, or fail to, understand the assertion. 'Indubitable' therefore means doubtable only at risk of infecting the sense of perceptual talk itself.

The notion here of a meaning-connection between evidence, as the assertibility condition for a perceptual claim, and any such claim itself, is something similar to Wittgenstein's notion of a criterion.[15] Precisely what Wittgenstein meant by 'criterion' is the special province of an extensive exegetical industry and still *sub judice*, so it would be foolish to claim more than a degree of co-belligerence on this head between Wittgenstein's views and those being urged here. However, to talk of criteria and a 'criterial relation' in at least the same spirit as Wittgenstein is informative. Earlier it was noted that on an antirealist approach, understanding sentences is to know how to recognise when one is warranted in using them. Evidently, of

[14] See C. Phillips, 'Constructivism and epistemology', *Philosophy* 53 (1978), for a very interesting discussion, on which I gratefully draw here.

[15] Cf. *Philosophical Investigations*, e.g. 143-6, 172-8, 182-4.

course, the kind of warrant at issue is such as neither to *entail* the claim, nor to stand to the claim as *inductive* warrant, for what one recognises as warranting use of a particular sentence is that these are the conditions for the sense of the sentence, and this does not constitute an entailment-relation (for *p* is defeasible to the extent permitted by the theory of error implicit in our grasp of the language); but yet is stronger than merely contingent conditions fixing the sentence's epistemic value. That this latter is the case may be seen by considering an example (the example is drawn from Phillips, p. 55). A chemical experiment is conducted by X in which a piece of blue litmus paper is immersed in a solution S. It turns red, and X concludes that S is acidic. Y, observing the experiment, does not see why this should follow. But X is justified in holding S to be acidic, for this just is one of the ways we are justified in saying that S is acidic – it has turned blue litmus paper red. Evidently it is not that Y fails to understand 'S is acidic'. He may indeed be well able to give an account of what an acid is; it may just be that he does not know about the effect of acid on litmus paper. Accordingly, understanding a sentence must consist in a grasp of what would *non-inductively* justify asserting it; we should not say that anyone does not understand a sentence only because he lacks such information as could inductively justify its use. Possession of warrant for the use of a sentence may then be informatively described as consisting in the knowledge that the evidence is a *criterion* for the use of the sentence. The usefulness of employing such a notion is clear. What the sceptic wishes to know is what account can be given of *evidence* given that the justification we have for asserting *p* on the basis of *e* is just that *e* is evidence for *p*. *E*'s being evidence for *p* is either a contingent or a necessary matter; if *e* is contingently evidence for *p*, we could only come to know that it is *evidence* for *p* by experience; but this renders our notion of evidence vulnerable to sceptical attack. By contrast, if grasping the sense of *p is* to know that *e* is evidence for it, that is, that *e* is the (or a) criterion for *p*, then it is necessary that *e* is evidence for *p* – we know that *e* is evidence for *p* a priori (Phillips, p. 56). Learning a language is, crucially, to learn *when* saying *what* is appropriate; to talk of a criterial ('meaning-connection') relation between occasions for the use of sentences and those sentences themselves is to say that we do not discover *post facto* that these sentences are assertible in these circumstances; it is just too difficult to see how, if this is how things are, anyone could ever come by a language. But denying that we know the assertibility-conditions for sentences only a posteriori is not to deny that we are ever wrong, as the fact that there is a theory of error written into the sense-conditions of the language (strictly, fragment of language) allows and even demands.

For any ordinary perceptual judgment – for example 'the tablecloth is blue' – matters are therefore like this: the statement is assertible because we know – in virtue of understanding the language – in what kinds of perceptual circumstances we would be warranted in asserting it. This means that we know two kinds of interdependent things; we know which terms are systematically correlated by a rule to such and such items or features of our experience, and we know what it is to recognise those items or features. Knowing these two things provides us with principles of this sort: 'When matters are like this in my experience, I am perceiving a tablecloth' (and so for '... a blue tablecloth' or any manageably complex experience which could be standardly so described). On a given occasion, when our experience is such that we recognise it *as* a case when matters are like this in our experience, we are entitled to say 'This is a (blue) tablecloth'. If there is any relevant reason for doubting our entitlement to assert such a statement, we can check for defeating counter-evidence by ticking off the list in our implicit theory of error. Could the light be misleading me? Am I drunk? Was I dreaming? And so on. In most normal cases we do not have to correct ourselves, and in most cases of our having to correct ourselves we do not have to make much effort to do so; *mistakes* are themselves readily defeasible. For the most part, however, in making perceptual judgments we are simply confident that *this* is how things are, because *this* is what perceiving a blue tablecloth consists in and what saying 'This is a blue tablecloth' 'means'.

It has been argued[16] that perceptual evidence, offered in statements about the way things look, can only justify statements about the way things are if they do so in the presence of some independent principle, thus: 'The tablecloth is blue' is supported by 'The tablecloth looks blue' only if we hold that 'Things that look like this in these circumstances are tablecloths and are blue'; and that there must be some way of establishing the principle which is not question-begging. What is imputed above to anyone who

[16] R.J. Fogelin *Evidence and Meaning*, London 1967, pp. 94-8.

understands perceptual talk is a grasp of such principles; his grasp of them consists in having the two interdependent pieces of knowledge specified. Such principles are, in effect, statements of the sense-conditions for the sentences in question.

If it is objected that it is at least misleading to say that someone who understands perceptual talk *knows* these two interdependent things, there is this manoeuvre to make: the knowledge being imputed to him need only be characterised as *implicit* knowledge. Two things need to be specified in an ascription of implicit knowledge of this sort – what it is someone implicitly knows (which is the matter under discussion), and in what his possession of it consists, that is, what would count as his manifesting such knowledge.[17] The latter is a straightforward matter; a person manifests his implicit knowledge of the conditions of sense for a discourse if he uses the discourse properly, which is at lest to say, consonantly with the usage of his linguistic community.

Now, what is crucial to this account of the conditions of sense is the perceiver's recognising items and features in his experience, and recognising them as (if this is different) those items and features to which certain terms apply. There is little to be gained from giving a psychologistic account (as Quine does) of how anyone as a matter of fact comes to make the discriminations among his experiences which enable him to identify and reidentify the items and features over which his discourse ranges, nor how as a matter of fact he comes to share the community's discourse, although for an account of reference we need to suppose a little psychological history in order to make sense of ostension (or something like it).[18] Instead what is needed is an account of what, given that the sense of perceptual talk demands that we are able to discriminate items and features in our experience, and correlate terms of our perceptual discourse with them, explains these capacities. It is important to recall that these capacities are necessary conditions for perceptual talk, for, clearly, there would be no sense in having a perceptual discourse if the items over which it purported to range were inscrutable in some way, that is, if we were not able to pick them out and later reidentify them. *And this is precisely the crucial point*: for what explains the capacity to make

[17] Cf. M.A.E. Dummett, 'What is a Theory of Meaning? II', pp. 70-1.

[18] An argument from the necessary intersubjectivity of language could be cultivated from this point, but I shall not take this tack here.

perceptual judgments is our commitment to believing that there are *objects*; that is, that the candidates we take to be the individuable and reidentifiable topics of perceptual discourse are propertied spatio-temporal continuants existing independently of our perception of them.

So much is pre-theoretically obvious, and its obviousness is what makes one feel in advance that sceptical doubts are misguided. The claim that needs to be made out here is that belief in the existence of such objects is a necessary condition of our having coherent experience (senseful discourse). The argument looks to be a promising one: if perceptual talk is to be senseful, then it must be possible for us to discriminate and reidentify objects, for otherwise we should not have the capacity to recognise that matters are such in our experience for our use of sentences correlated with such experiences to be warranted; indeed, we should not be able to set up the correlations on which assertibility conditions in general rest. Both in connection with assertibility conditions in general, i.e. knowing which terms correlate with which states of affairs in our experience, and in connection with recognising that a particular set of experiences warrants us in use of a particular sentence, or set of them, on a particular occasion, demand that we take it that our experiences and our talk are addressed to a public domain of objects.

Assumptions to the effect that there are objects therefore, and obviously, underlie both perception and perceptual talk. In saying that the sense of perceptual talk is secured by a presupposition to the effect that there is something that perceptual talk refers to, and that we take it that there are objects and states of affairs we can recognise and our recognition of which warrants our actual use of such terms, we are saying that the assumption of objects is *fundamental* to both perception and perceptual discourse. It is in this way that perceptual judgments are 'internal' to a conceptual scheme which provides the justification for the perceptual beliefs to which we commit ourselves in making such judgments: the scheme has it that there are objects, and that both our talk and perceivings refer to them and are both intelligible only as *both* referring to them. This is, as it were, a principle governing perceptual judgment: a schematic representation would run something like this – statements *e* of the evidence for some perceptual statement *p* are always made on the basis of (or 'in the presence of') a general assumption or principle A to the effect that *e* determines the sense of *p*'; one is warranted in asserting *p* because

(A)*e*. This is analogous to cases of nomological relations between universal laws and initial conditions, on the one hand, and those conclusions which, on the other hand, can be deduced from their conjunction. But perceptual judgments are not nomological, only nomological-like. For A implicitly contains an account of *e*'s defeasibility (the theory of error), and *ipso facto* cannot in conjunction with *e* entail *p*. Rather, the relation of *e* to *p* is best construed as follows: in the linguistic mode, (A)*e* constitute the conditions of sense for *p*; in the material mode, the beliefs to which *p* gives expression are justified by the beliefs to which A and *e* give expression. *E*-type beliefs are particular perceptual beliefs like *p*-type beliefs; A-beliefs are transcendental beliefs. I shall return to this point.

Our perceptual experience can be characterised only by means of expressions which carry essential reference to the objects over which we take it to range; this is a point established earlier. The sensefulness of perceptual talk and the intelligibility, order, or coherence of our experience are accordingly matters which run *pari passu*. Arguments to the essential connectedness of perceptual talk and experience can be shown by such considerations as these: one can argue that if certain statements are to count as expressing the evidence for what is claimed in some further statement, then our experience must be so ordered that we can rely upon it to legitimise the belief expressed by the further statement. For example, (a) 'Here are some fresh fox spoor' allows us to conclude (b) 'There is a fox nearby'. Only if we can expect the right kind of regularities in our experience will (a) license (b); in a world where fresh fox-spoor appear on many or most occasions without help from foxes, (a) and (b) could not connect in the relevant way. Again, if 'There is a mahogany kneehole desk in the next room' is to be a senseful statement, it must at least be that we can have experiences which are all and only characterisable as experiences of mahogany kneehole desks, and it must be possible that there could be one in the next room. The possibility in question must, further, be an empirically realisable one; we must be able to encounter such things (desks) in such arrangements ('being in the next room') in our experience. What these considerations show is this: questions about the intelligibility or coherence of our experience, and questions about the sensefulness of our discourse, are at bottom equivalent. (From the point of view of human experience, this is not contentious; a difficulty arises if the issue is construed generally, as one about the intelligibility of experience *tout court*. This is another point I shall return to.)

The discussion to this point is intended to show how the conditions of sense for our perceptual talk, i.e. the intelligibility of our perceptual experience, demand that we take it that our perceptual talk and experience addresses itself to an ontology of objects. So far, nothing has been shown about 'objects' beyond the fact that they are items which we take to exist independently of our talk and perception, and that there are some sort of connections between at least some of them. It is also implicit in what has so far been said that they are spatio-temporal continuants, as defined earlier. The looseness of this characterisation allows that the standard accusatives of perceptions and perceptual talk might best be construed as features or events rather than particulars, although nothing much turns on these nicer ontological distinctions unless 'spatio-temporal continuant' will not do. It seems to me that it will, however, do.

All that the argument to this point establishes if it is right, however, is that the coherence of our perceptual talk and experience depends on the *assumption* that there is an external world, for being bound to employ objectivity concepts does not of itself entail that anything answers to those concepts, as can be shown by considering a possible ideal universe of experience. Concepts of what we would ordinarily discriminate as 'subjective' and 'objective' elements in experience could be characterised in an idealist account as belonging to different conceptual categories, such that concepts in the O 'objective' category (tables, stones) differ from those in the S 'subjective' category (memories, desires) in virtue of some such features as that O-concepts are, say, far less tractable to one's willings than S-concepts; that they are linked together in more determinate fashion than S-concepts, in such a way that their connections are lawlike; that thoughts intending O-type accusatives differ in quality from those intending S-type ones – for example, in Humean fashion, by being more 'vivid', say – and so on. In such an ideal universe of experience the perceiver must be able to discriminate between O-type and S-type concepts, and does so by means of the criteria sketched, and others; he may well refer

O-concepts to an external reality for simplicity. It does not follow that there is an external reality. This sketch of an idealist experience is not of course offered as an exhaustive one; it is merely a gesture in the direction of showing that possession of objectivity concepts and their applicability in experience does not entail that there are objects. It is a case exactly parallel to religious experience and discourse; the sense of a prayer in large part depends upon a commitment, by the one who prays, to the ontological effect that there is a God, from which it does not follow that there is God. *Explaining* what it is to pray, or what the prayerful man 'means' when he utters prayers, necessarily involves reference to the man's ontological presuppositions in the crucial respect; there can be no understanding of prayer and particular prayers otherwise. As in the idealist case, that certain conceptual discriminations are a necessary condition of the intelligibility of such an enterprise does not entail the truth of an ontology upon which such discriminations turn; as in the case of ordinary perceptual talk and experience, they are, however, no less necessary for all that.

The foregoing discussion can now be rounded off by remarking some of the features derived and by showing how it puts us in a position to meet scepticism at the proper level.

Perceptual beliefs were earlier characterised as beliefs about objects or states of affairs involving them in actual and possible perceptual environments (or on particular experiential occasions). 'The tablecloth is blue' expresses beliefs to the effect that here is a tablecloth and it is blue, which are beliefs of some sophistication, turning as they do on a grasp of classifications of objects and their properties of a kind that involves a wide range of other beliefs – other perceptual beliefs and general beliefs both. As the class of perceptual beliefs has been delimited here, it does not include beliefs about our acts of perception independently of their possible accusatives; talk of 'seeming' to see a blue tablecloth, or 'being appeared-to blue-tableclothly', constitutes a special attempt to axe the perceptual accusative and specify the content of our sensory state in isolation from it. This is intended to capture and capitalise upon a distinction made by Kant: the distinction, in his terminology, between judgments and purely subjective assertions (B142). The former involve objective reference *essentially*; that is, their conditions of sense turn upon our taking it that the terms employed refer to objects (thus we assume objects), and that we recognise them as the objects to which the terms refer; which means that we take it that we have perceptual access to those objects (and thus again, assume objects). Purely subjective assertions describe how things seem to me to be, whether or not they are so; a perceptual statement or judgment goes beyond this, and states that there are things which *are* thus and so. It is because perceptual statements do this that Ayer and others talked of them as 'going beyond the evidence' or as 'committing' us to an ontology underdetermined by 'the evidence'. The argument put here is that that commitment is carried by the discourse, and the experience it reports, *essentially*.

Perception and perceptual talk, and the characterisations of our sensory states which we effect by retreating from the ontological reference of perceptual talk, in this way rest upon a presupposition of objects. It is a presupposition of 'This is a blue tablecloth', when non-idly asserted, that there is an object, and it states that the object is to be classified as one of a certain kind having a certain property or quality. Since 'This is a blue tablecloth' is a perceptual statement expressing a perceiver's beliefs about a segment of his perceptual environment, the presupposed objective commitment is unproblematic. Thus, suppose a man is pointed out to me as 'the King of France', and I note that he is bald. Because in a report of my perceptual judgment that he is bald, namely 'the King of France is bald', I am using the description referentially in Donnellan's sense,[19] as one employed on a particular occasion on which I intend to pick out something by means of the description, the fact that there is no King of France will not affect the objective presupposition of the statement. Indeed, for any perceptual statement, a demonstrative could be substituted for the description, proper name or general term constituting the subject, in order to show what, *qua* perceptual statement, it is intended to convey: in the focal case, a perceptual statement expresses beliefs that there is something which is thus and so at a given time, and the intention to refer (that is, the assumption of the object) is in such cases most simple and direct.

The result of sketching conditions of sense for perceptual talk in

[19] K.S. Donnellan, 'Reference and definite descriptions' in Schwarz (ed.), *Naming, Necessity and Natural Kinds*, Ithaca 1977.

the foregoing way is wholly intuitive. We are inclined to say that in ordinary perceptual situations, our judgments, and the statements we make in reporting them (saving a *lapsus linguae*), can only be called in question either by someone who does not, or chooses not to, understand the language, or by the philosophical sceptic. And now we can notice two things: in the former case, that is, of someone who does not understand the language, or who chooses not to accept the 'language game', we explain what is going on – what his doubt comes down to – by talking in terms of the *sense* of the discourse at issue. In the latter case, it is crucially important to note that what the sceptic is concerned with is something of a different order, namely the issue of what justifies us in holding the beliefs implicit in our talk. He is fully prepared to accept that in the circumstances it is right to utter the sentence 'This is a blue tablecloth'; that is, he is not concerned to establish that 'this' is something different, like a red tablecloth or a blue toffee-apple; instead, he wants to know how, if at all, we are justified in holding that there *is* a 'this', or anything else, at all. The foregoing shows how the sceptic's request is to be met: by showing that the objective assumptions of perceptual talk and experience are essential to their intelligibility. Showing this constitutes a reply to scepticism; if objective assumptions are necessary, then even if it cannot be further shown that they are true, scepticism is defeated.

Some remarks on truth are called for here. In the foregoing, no notion of truth is employed, use being made instead of a notion of warrant, regarded as wholly verification-dependent; and warrant is characterisable as what attaches to an utterer's use of a statement when he has grounds on that occasion of utterance for it. It is important to note this: a statement like 'the dome of St Paul's Cathedral will be visible above the roofs of Fleet Street in A.D. 3000' is assertible (we know what perceptual situations its constituent terms can be employed in and what states of affairs the sentence as a whole could be employed in), but until 3000 A.D. it cannot be warranted, because the relevant actual perceptual situation is not available to us. Accordingly, since it is probable to some degree that that situation will become available, the statement is itself probable to that degree. I would suggest on the basis of this, but shall not argue the matter here, (a) that statements about the past, future or elsewhere are always probable to some degree for an utterer on an occasion, (b) that statements about his present perceptual environment are alone what can in the right circumstances be undefeatedly warranted and (c), since matters can be put like this, the terms 'true' and 'false' are redundant in a philosophical account of perceptual talk and experience. 'True' and 'false' undoubtedly have several useful roles in ordinary discourse, and certain specific roles in formal contexts; but if the foregoing account is right, then at least for the issues in hand these notions are eliminable.

These remarks may seem to contradict a claim about a matter so fundamental that they cannot be allowed to pass too quickly. I am disinclined to think that this is so. In talking of the justification-conditions for the perceptual claims we ordinarily make, we are attempting to show when and why our beliefs entitle us to make the empirical judgments we are accustomed to make daily. This is the same thing as tracing out the structure of our beliefs and showing how, by virtue of their structure, they bear the weight of our epistemological claims; under constraint of requirements of consistency or coherence among these; a belief-structure which can be shown to justify our ordinary claims is thus far *rational*. Now, it is a standard view that rational systems of belief are rational just in virtue of their being truth-directed, and successfully so, and that the rules by means of which beliefs can be seen truth-directedly to support – or otherwise variously relate to – one another, are the rules of logic. Truth theories, indeed, form the basis of logical systems, which is why, on the standard view of these matters, truth is regarded as the fundamental notion for understanding justification described under species of the rationality of a belief system. On this view, then, knowledge of truth-conditions is something we must have before we can talk about justification or warrant. A certain plausibility attaches to this view on the face of it, for we know that we cannot hold both the belief that, say, something is green and nothing is green in the same system of beliefs, and that knowing this derives from our knowing the truth-conditions for the sentences 'Some particular thing is green' and 'Nothing is green'. But despite this appearance of plausibility in behalf of the truth-conditional approach, matters are otherwise. We can recognise a system of beliefs as rational – that is, as consistent and as having relations of consequence or support between its members – without being able to furnish an adequate specification of the truth-conditions for the sentences expressing those beliefs; indeed, it is not even necessary to our recognising that some belief is justified on the basis of certain others, or that two or more beliefs are consistent or inconsistent with respect to one another, that we believe the sentences expressing the beliefs to be true or false (still less 'objectively' true or false). Thus an account of justification can be given without depending on an assumption to the effect that understanding truth is crucially prior to understanding justification. It is in this sense that the notion of truth is eliminable, for what is to be understood as truth is more than adequately usurped by talk, instead, of warrant. Indeed in view of the obscurity which attaches to the notion of truth, its replacement by the more perspicuous idiom of warrant marks an advance in its own right.

The central point of the foregoing may now be recapitulated schematically. The thrust of scepticism is that there is a gap between the evidence we have for claims about the world, on the one hand, and that evidence itself on the other. My argument here is that this gap is closed by the context in which evidence for claims is couched, the context being the framework of transcendental beliefs which underpin our thought and talk. The evidence for our claims is internal to a conceptual scheme whose basis is the transcendental beliefs; it is the internality of the evidence to the scheme which, together with the theory of error written into our understanding of evidence, provides justification for our particular empirical judgments and our verbal reports and assertions of them. Scepticism about any particular empirical judgment is thus defeated by appeal to the fact that the judgment is made in terms of the scheme; what it means to say that a judgment is unwarranted is that the scheme does not support it, but this is something which it is only possible to say because it is also possible to say when, relative to the scheme, a judgment *is* warranted.

But this does not defeat scepticism, although it defeats scepticism at the level at which it has traditionally been pitched. The sceptic will now raise his sights and attack the notions of transcendental beliefs and what justifies them – such as the notion of a conceptual scheme, and of the propriety of the arguments used to show what is fundamental to it. The next two chapters develop a defence against this higher level scepticism.

CHAPTER THREE

'Conceptual Schemes' and Relativism

The point of the last chapter was to show how particular perceptual claims are justified on the grounds that they are made within the context of a conceptual scheme, fundamental to which are certain beliefs necessarily presupposed by all thought and talk constituting the scheme. Showing this meets the sceptical challenge for a demonstration of the justification conditions for ordinary empirical judgments. It does not, however, meet the sceptical challenge conclusively; for the sceptic can now respond by raising questions about the justifying apparatus introduced.

If empirical judgments are made within the justifying context of a conceptual scheme to which there is presupposed a set of transcendentally necessary beliefs, then the sceptic will regard it as crucially important to ask, What is a conceptual scheme? Moreover, is there only one conceptual scheme, or are there many? If there are many, and if each (or even quite a few) of them putatively presuppose different transcendental beliefs, then appeal to conceptual schemes and their underpinnings of transcendental beliefs does not in the end justify ordinary empirical judgments, because the fact of their *relativity* with respect to a conceptual scheme will be the opposite of epistemologically compelling.

These sceptical thoughts about the notion of a conceptual scheme concern not only the matter of how the notion is itself to be understood, but also the issue of relativism, which involves considerations of some complexity. Evidently, if the sceptic's doubts about the notion of a conceptual scheme are going to be settled satisfactorily, what must be substantiated, in addition to giving a suitable characterisation of the notion, is the claim that all conceptual schemes have the same specifiable fundamental structure with respect to the nature and organisation of empirical experience.

If the sceptic is answered satisfactorily on the foregoing, there remain equally if not more vital questions which he can urge against the justifying apparatus proposed in the last chapter. These concern the nature of transcendental arguments, and whether, and if so how, they are valid; and of course the central demand is for an explicit characterisation and defence of the transcendental arguments employed in the course of this argument.

In this chapter I shall deal with the questions concerning the notion of a conceptual scheme and relativism; in the next I shall deal with transcendental arguments.

It might appear that there is a ready defence against the sceptic's doubts concerning the notion of a conceptual scheme, a defence which, if it works, would obviate the necessity for discussing the matter at all. This defence is to appeal to Carnap's distinction between 'internal' and 'external' questions,[1] which allows us to say that because ordinary perceptual claims are justified in virtue of their inherence in a scheme or framework, and because questions about schemes or framework themselves, being 'external' questions, concern only the practical matter of whether or not to adopt them, sceptical doubts about our ordinary everyday conceptual scheme as a whole (the 'framework of things' as Carnap calls it, p. 206) are misguided. This issue is worth discussing in some detail because it raises a number of relevant points.

Carnap's proposals are in some important respects attractive from the point of view of the argument here, but they do not afford the ready escape from sceptical doubts suggested. Why this is so may be seen from an inspection of what Carnap argues.

What is common ground between Carnap's views and those being urged here concerns the validation of claims about spatio-temporal things and events; on both views, as noted, such claims are made within the context of a framework and derive their justification-conditions from that fact. Questions about such claims are thus 'internal'. In sharp contrast, as Carnap views it, 'external' questions about the framework – most important, as to whether the system of

[1] R. Carnap, 'Empiricism, semantics, and ontology' in *Meaning and Necessity*, Chicago 1956, pp. 205ff.

things is as a whole real – cannot ever be resolved, because they are wrongly formulated. 'To be real in the scientific sense means to be an element of the system; hence this concept cannot be meaningfully applied to the system itself' (ibid.). Accordingly, questions about the system as a whole must be practical rather than theoretical ones, having to do with decisions concerning the structure of the thing world language, and whether or not to accept and employ these or those of its forms of expression. Although, in the case of the thing world, 'there is usually no deliberate choice because we all have accepted the thing language early in our lives' (ibid.), it is still open to us to choose whether or not to continue using it; on Carnap's view, it is open to us to construct an alternative thing language, or to restrict ourselves to a purely phenomenal language. But if in accepting the thing-language we can be said to have 'accepted the world of things', this must not be taken to mean that we have accepted 'a *belief* in the reality of the thing world', for 'there is no such belief or assertion or assumption, because it is not a theoretical question. To accept the thing world means nothing more than to accept a certain form of language' (pp. 206-7). Carnap has it that our acceptance and use of the thing language will turn upon its efficiency, fruitfulness and simplicity relative to its purpose, which is communication. These features do not, in Carnap's view, entitle us to say that, in view of its efficacy, the language confirms the reality of the thing world; all that this entitles us to say is that we are well advised to use the language. Having 'accepted' the form of language in question, we are entitled to assert and believe particular claims, such as (Carnap's example) 'There is a white piece of paper on my desk'. According to Carnap, recognising something 'as a real thing or event means to succeed in incorporating it into the system of things at a particular space-time position so that it fits together with the other things recognised as real, according to the rules of the framework' (p. 206). The upshot of Carnap's view is that I can assert and believe a claim and be justified by the scheme in doing so; but I cannot assert or believe that the scheme overall is anything other than a purely conventional one, adopted for pragmatic reasons only and in principle replaceable by an alternative scheme.

There are several reasons why this view of Carnap's will not do. What is crucial to his position is his proposed analysis of 'real' – 'To be real ... is to be an element of the system' – and the consequences of this for the problem of justification, which problem is the focus of the sceptic's challenge. Carnap's motive for wishing to construe reality as a system-relative property is that, in connection with mathematical and physical theories, the entities belonging to them cease to pose ontological problems altogether if the proposal is accepted. Now, whether there is enough in common between such theories on the one hand and our everyday conceptual scheme on the other to permit the univocal application of Carnap's view to both seems very doubtful. One central consideration is the degree to which there is in fact a choice about our thing language in the sense in which there can be choices, on the grounds of simplicity, predictive power and the like, between alternative scientific theories. Carnap, as noted, remarks that 'there is usually no deliberate choice because we all have accepted the thing language early in our lives', which leaves it open that later deliberate choices can be made, and that having a thing language of the sort we do is a wholly contingent matter. The natural reaction to this is trenchantly put by Quinton: 'But really the whole idea of proposing and deciding to adopt or reject such massive tracts of our conceptual apparatus as the thing-language or the number-system is impossible to accept. These are not open questions.'[2] The reason why these are not open questions is the interesting issue, and it is to this precise issue that the overall argument here is addressed. In application to Carnap's views matters can be put like this.

There is a short answer to Carnap, proffered by Stroud.[3] It is that, despite Carnap's attempt to smother or extinguish the sceptical problem, the notion of alternative frameworks is simply implausible, and it remains that the external question seems to be perfectly intelligible and compelling, and in need of an answer. This seems to me right as far as it goes, but it does not go far. There are deeper worries, as follows.

If in considering our everyday framework of things the internal-external dichotomy is accepted as settling what counts as real, then the distinction between what *is* the case and what *seems* to be the case will be a strictly framework-relative notion, the result being that in a possible alternative scheme matters could be such

[2] A.M. Quinton, *The Nature of Things*, London 1975, p. 248.

[3] B. Stroud, 'The significance of scepticism' in *Transcendental Arguments and Science*, Dordrecht 1979.

that what *seems* will be what *is*, and what *is* what *seems*. This is a 'weak' is-seems distinction owing to its parochiality with respect to a framework. Now, if terms of epistemic valuation are to have uniform senses, there must be satisfiable criteria of application for them, such that there would be a way of showing across closely related frameworks that these and those items play the role, or do not play the role, in framework A which they play in framework B (presumably this is part of how one would distinguish frameworks). But this suggests a 'strong' is-seems distinction, a distinction which gives rise to our pre-theoretical sense of what is the case objectively or independently of our choices, and what is subjective or to be classified just in terms of our interests and purposes. How do we make sense of a strong is-seems distinction on Carnap's terms, given that the weak is-seems distinction he allows itself falls into the second class – that is, the class of subjectively determined concepts chosen to suit our interests and purposes?

The problem is thrown more starkly into relief when we consider that, if a strong is-seems distinction is not available, we cannot go so far as to set up a concept of objectivity which is faithful to our pre-theoretical intuitions.[4] Presumably Carnap would regard this as a virtue of his proposal, for sceptical doubts about objectivity, in the form of doubts about whether there are things or a world existing objectively, that is, independently of our thought and talk, are precisely doubts of the sort Carnap wishes to rule out *ex hypothesi* as 'cognitively senseless' (op. cit., p. 211), on the grounds that they are 'prior' or external to the framework. But if we have no concept of objectivity because we have no way of formulating a strong is-seems distinction, then neither do we have a concept of subjectivity – the concept (in this epistemological context) crucial to any understanding of experience; and therefore we have no concept of experience. (Experience is not, on Carnap's view (p. 209) framework-relative; only what it ranges over.) For, whatever else experience consists in, giving an account of it cannot proceed by way of a no-ownership thesis for experience; someone or something must have or enjoy experience, which is demanded by what Strawson calls the 'necessary self-reflexiveness' (op. cit., p. 107) by which any experience must be characterised. For something to be experience,

[4] Cf. for example R. Scruton, 'Objectivity and the will', *Mind* 82 (1973), for some related thoughts.

that is, it must be owned by a subject able to recognise that the experience is his own, and this is possible only on condition that there is 'room', as Strawson puts it, 'for the thought of experience itself' (ibid.). The mutual dependence of the is-seems distinction and the concepts of objectivity, subjectivity and experience can be displayed readily: in order for there to be experience, it must be self-reflexive, which is to say it must be recognised by a subject as belonging to itself, which in turn demands that the subject has a concept of the objective (of what, strongly, *is* independently of how things *seem* to itself). Consequently any view, such as Carnap's, which rules out a strong is-seems distinction renders the concept of experience unintelligible and therefore unavailable. It follows from this that Carnap's view, and by extension any view specifying that talk of things is to be understood as talk only of the entities demanded by a selected language of things, looks to be, by *reductio*, contradictory. For Carnap is seeking to satisfy empiricist scruples about abstract entities, that is, non-concrete entities, entities not to be met with in perceptual experience; and he makes central use of a notion of observationality, by talking of how the things constituted as real by the thing-framework are fitted into their places in the framework by 'empirical investigations' (op. cit., p. 207). A concept of experience is crucial to talk not only of the empirical procedures of observation, but of course to understanding what is meant by 'empirical' itself.

Another way of putting this difficulty about Carnap's views, given the reliance they place on observation, is that one of the compelling phenomenological facts about what we take to be the objects (= *objective* accusatives; not just accusatives) of our experience, is their intransigence and their 'haecceity'; they lie there, as it were, to be observed and at times even discovered, and it is for the most part by consulting them (as opposed to our decisions regarding how to talk of them) that we settle questions arising in connection with them. The proposal that what is real is what is an element of the system, and that the system is a matter of choice, offends against the insistently felt objectivity of the world of things, which, even if it turned out to be a radically misguided intuition, needs to be accounted for in some way. Providing such an account would show why it would be (*if* it is) silly to respond to Carnap's view by saying: if you don't like this world of things you can choose another language with a different ontology. On the face of it it is very likely that whereas one is free to choose a different language, two related facts would make any language-changing enterprise *ontologically* pointless: what there is in the perceived world would still be there, and the new language and the old would intertranslate. The relation between these two facts will be one of dependence, leaving aside for the moment the question of the dependence's direction (see below). These are matters I shortly discuss in more detail, for what is looming large here is the issue of relativism.

Taking it that our choice of language is arbitrary plays directly into the hands of the sceptic. His question concerns what justification we have for believing that there are objects, and on Carnap's terms the answer is – none, if you are thinking of objects in some full-blooded sense as independent of our thought and talk; otherwise if you accept a system-relative notion of what is real, the framework justifies our ordinary beliefs because they are internal to it. If the sceptic then asks his higher-level sceptical question, the Kant question of 'Quid juris'? with respect to the framework, and the answer comes that we could choose whatever framework we cared for, then scepticism is vindicated; this is precisely the kind and degree of relativism which would satisfy the sceptic that in the end there is no justification for our beliefs, because relative justification could precisely be one of a sceptic's options for an agnoiological epistemology.

A difficulty for my own purposes here might appear to rise from these considerations. One of the chief attractions of realism is that it opposes facts of the matter to language so that language, or at any rate its assertoric constituents, can be true of them. Earlier, in connection with the discussion of sense conditions for perceptual talk, I gave reasons for rejecting a realist approach.[5] If one rejects realism, however, it is not immediately clear what one's concept of objectivity consists in, and it makes it more difficult to see how relativism is to be resisted – if, indeed, it *can* be resisted by an antirealist. In

[5] Cf. Chapter 2 above. I am again taking the view that questions of language and questions of ontology are so intimately linked that one can employ the now standard labels 'realism' and 'anti-realism' for either set of questions about the external world or perceptual talk without reiterating fine qualifications. Both labels of course apply only to given classes of statements; the class at issue here is that of perceptual statements.

rejecting Carnap's proposals, both a concept of objectivity and a promised counter to relativism have been employed. Some account must be given, therefore, to resolve these apparent tensions.

These tensions may be thrown into sharp relief as follows. Two of the important strands in the entire argument here are (1) that the way we[6] think and talk about the world is not arbitrary, and indeed is so far from arbitrary that all conceptual schemes share the same basic features with respect to the organisation of experience, which features, in view of their nature and role, are transcendentally necessary to experience; and (2) that these features consist in realist assumptions about the objects of perceptual thought and talk, namely that they exist independently of such thought and talk. These theses suggest that adopting realism with respect to the world of experience and the discourse which ranges over it is natural and appropriate. The tension arises from the fact that I do not adopt realism, for the reasons given earlier, and thus I appear to block the availability of an appeal to matters of fact, opposed and prior to language, to flesh out a concept of objectivity by means of which to reject Carnap's views.

The appearance of strain between these aspects of the argument disappears when it is recognised that a claim to the effect that certain realist assumptions are transcendentally necessary to experience is not equivalent to the claim that realism with respect to the objects of experience is true. Whereas the former claim can be made out by transcendental argument, as it is my intention to show, the latter claim cannot be made out.[7] This just says that showing that a presumption of objects is required by experience if that experience is to be coherent, is not equivalent to saying, nor does it entail, that there are objects independent of experience. I take this to be the force of Kant's distinction between 'transcendental realism' and 'transcendental idealism', to which I shall revert later.[8] The claim is that experience demands that there be objects. The realist's claim is that there are objects. In one sense, the difference between the two claims is very small; if experience demands that there be objects, then, because there is experience, there are objects, which is the

[6] For suitable 'we', cf. below.

[7] Cf. Chapter 1 above and Chapter 4 below. The difference between what I am arguing here and what Carnap argued will, despite appearances, shortly emerge.

[8] Cf. Kant, op. cit., A367 (the Fourth Paralogism) and Chapter 4 below.

realist's claim too. But the appearance of conformity is superficial, for the realist's claim is that there are objects independently of anyone's ever experiencing them, whereas the claim I am making is, simply, that it does not make sense to say this. The realist's claim, in literally making no sense, is thus not false; for to claim that it is false would be to enter into a dispute about whether there are or not, *per impossible* in some absolute sense, 'really' or 'actually' or 'in fact' objects. Such a dispute is wholly idle because 'There are objects independently of experience' is not assertible; it is like someone's saying 'I see an invisible cup', the remedy for which is not a quarrel over whether he in fact sees the invisible cup or not, but assistance with his understanding the language. The question is therefore not whether there are objects in some absolute sense, but whether it would be possible to make intelligible a notion of experience which does not rely upon a distinction between subjects and objects of experience. For the reasons given earlier (Chapter 2), the answer is negative; talk of experience carries essential reference to objects, and cannot be understood otherwise. This has the appropriate result that we can reject Carnap's view on the grounds that it does not allow a strong distinction between what is and what seems, which distinction is necessary to understanding experience, without thereby being forced to accept realism; a line is navigated between the Scylla and Charybdis of equally untenable positions. As regards Carnap's views, what is being rejected is not the idea that the scheme demands objects, for so it does; rather, it is the idea that there are alternative schemes not demanding objects or demanding different objects, which we could choose to adopt if we so wished.

This captures, in part, the sense of Kant's claim that there are certain features of experience fundamental to all experience; but only in part, for nothing does or can follow from the truth of this, if it *is* true, that such features in some way reflect how things 'absolutely', 'in fact', or 'really' are independently of all experience – which is to say, not only does the truth of Kant's claim carry no entailment to the truth of a realist point of this kind, but nothing *could* count as establishing its truth; we cannot step outside our scheme to see whether it accurately reflects the way things (absolutely) are behind or beyond it – no veil of perception or conception is at issue here, which explains why the truth, if it is true, of Kant's claim does not entitle us to invoke any kind of noumenon, a point Kant himself has often and justly been charged with failing to see.[9]

Showing in more detail how to dispense with the relativist implications of Carnap's view, while remaining in a position to use the notion of a scheme or framework as part of an anti-sceptical argument, rests mainly upon making out the notion of schemes or frameworks properly. I turn now to consider this notion, and to show in more detail how charges of relativism arising in connection with it are to be rejected.

The notion of conceptual schemes has gained wide currency in philosophical discussions of the last two decades, owing chiefly to the use made of it by Quine and Strawson.[10] In the latter's work the notion is regarded as self-explanatory, while Quine treats conceptual schemes in all important respects as theories; the 'immemorial doctrine' (our everyday conceptual scheme) is taken by Quine on all fours with theories in the particular sense that, like them, it admits of canonical paraphrase in a way revealing of its ontological implications. Nothing like a precise specification of the idea of a conceptual scheme, is, however, available in these sources; it has a persistent air of metaphor about it. Davidson identifies variations in the metaphor; conceptual schemes are '... ways of organising experience ... systems of categories that give form to the data of sense ... points of view from which individuals, cultures, or periods survey the passing scene'.[11] Characterisations at this level of generality turn on no more than our intuitive grasp of what the expression 'conceptual scheme', and its forerunners like 'world-view', *weltanschauung*, or even 'metaphysic', are intended to mean.

The vagueness of the notion may arise from antecedent vaguenesses concerning the constituent ideas of concepts and schemes, but it is more likely to arise from the fact that there is, given synchronic and diachronic variations respectively within and between general 'points of view', an inherent indeterminacy in what is to count at any given time as the conceptual scheme of a

[9] This issue of objectivity is canvassed again, with more materials to hand, in Chapter 4 below.

[10] Cf. W.V. Quine, *Word and Object*, New York, 1960, ch. 7; P.L. Strawson, *Individuals*, London 1959, esp. p. 71, ch. 1.

[11] D. Davidson, 'On the very idea of a conceptual scheme,' *Proceedings of the American Philsophical Association* (1974).

community of subscribers to it. My aims against relativism notwithstanding, variation and differences in 'world-views' certainly have to be admitted as an historical and cultural datum at least above the level of *transcendental* concepts; so much is obvious upon the merest inspection of the constrasts between, say, medieval and contemporary cosmologies. Other examples are legion. That this is so may appear to be cause for pessimism. Can the notion of a conceptual scheme be given enough detail and precision to bear the weight I am placing on it here? Davidson's views happily and interestingly suggest that it can, and accordingly I shall discuss them in some detail.

First, however, something needs to be noted about the scope of the expression 'conceptual scheme'. Evidently the focus of interest in considering conceptual schemes as forms of organisation of experience is what *our* thought and talk is like, where 'our' picks out language-using humans; but at the same time there is the more general and fundamental question of what has to be the case for the possibility of *any* experience, and it needs to be settled whether, in investigating human language-using experience, the conceptual universals sought will be conceptual universals in the latter wholly inclusive sense too. The answer depends on what is to count as a conceptual scheme in general.

The issue here turns upon whether 'any possible experience' and 'any experience recognisable as such by us' are considered equivalent or not. It follows directly from antirealist scruples of the kind I have been guided by that the former expression must be analysed into the latter. Those who hold the converse, as does Mackie,[12] that is, that there may be forms of experience which we cannot conceive because of mere limitations upon the imaginative faculty of humans, or because there is nothing contradictory about the notion of forms of experience unknown or unknowable to us, do so on the grounds that there must be a determinate truth-condition which 'there are forms of experience inconceivable and/or unconceived by humans' satisfies or fails to satisfy. Such a view is however untenable. What, after all, is to be understood by 'concept'? At least we should be able to say what counts as *possession* of a

[12] Cf. J.L. Mackie, *The Cement of the Universe*, Oxford 1974, ch. 4 passim, esp. pp. 96ff.

concept, and this is to be done by saying that whoever or whatever possesses a certain concept displays mastery of a practice in which is manifested an ability to make appropriate discriminations and responses of a variety of sorts.[13] Thus it is on the basis of someone's or something's (X's) ability to classify or recognise items, or being able to report, reason about, describe, or by some means 'locate' or differentially pick out, some item, that we attribute to X possession of the concept of the item. To take an easy case; for a *person* to be said to possess the concept of redness, he must be recognised as knowing how to use the word 'red'. This states a sufficient (but not a necessary) condition for ascription to him of mastery of the concept. Moreover, possession of a concept demands possession of further concepts. To have the concept of redness is, necessarily, to have a concept of colour in general; being able to apply 'red' to all and only red surfaces entails an ability to withhold 'red' in the presence of all and only non-red surfaces, and thus to discriminate, at the very least, two different colours. Because therefore we should find it impossible to ascribe possession of just one concept to X, attributing possession of a concept to X involves recognising that X possesses, however rudimentarily, a *scheme* of concepts, that is, a non-arbitrary arrangement of concepts by means of which arrangement he is able correctly to apply individual concepts in the scheme. X's manifesting possession of a particular concept thus entitles us to ascribe possession of such further concepts as are necessary for X's mastery of the practice in which possession of the first concept is displayed. The force of 'scheme' accordingly goes further than a mere cluster of related concepts; we would, on this basis, be entitled to hold that certain concepts are logically prior to others, that relations of dependence and consequence hold between the components of the scheme, and that if X's experience is anything more than rudimentary then X must be aware of at least some of these relations in order to employ successfully such concepts as would be unemployable without grasp of the relevant logically antecedent ones.

If this is right, then it is a condition of our understanding 'conceptual scheme' in general that at least we are able to recognise when some X possesses a concept (and therefore a scheme of concepts); any X which does nothing recognisable in this way

[13] Cf. P. Geach, *Mental Acts*, London 1957, §5.

cannot be said to possess concepts, for nothing attaches *sense* to the idea that X may indeed possess concepts despite our being sealed-off from understanding what it means to say this of X in this or any similar case. This shows that anything which is to count as a conceptual scheme must be recognisable as such to us.

But this is not enough for our purposes overall, for a problem arises here as to what Xs can be. If Xs are language-users, then matters are straightforward; but there is the vexed issue of whether, for example, non-language users like chimpanzees and dogs can be said to have conceptual schemes, and, if so, what difference that makes to any claim about the universality of certain features of conceptual schemes. The problem can be put like this: in the case of language-users the phenomenon of concept-applying activity admits, as Bishop puts it, of a distinctive kind of rational explanation, which turns on our being able to say that any language-user applies concepts, in some cases at least, in a way which is to be correctly described as being done *for reasons known to him*; and the question arises as to how far this kind of account can be given of animals too, that is, of whether they have practical thoughts underwriting intentional action, which can properly be described as *reasons* for action.[14] Evidently they do have practical thoughts; a chimpanzee will use a stick to get an out-of-reach banana, and a dog will sit at the front gate waiting for his master's return. Such behaviour, on the foregoing criteria, licenses attribution of concepts and practical thoughts to them. Is this the same thing as saying that they do things for reasons known to themselves? It is here that the difficulty lies, for whereas it is reasonably clear that certain animals have (at least rudimentary) conceptual schemes, and behave purposively in manifesting their possession of them, it is not clear that they thereby manifest the conceptual complexity, richness of texture, and self-reflexive awareness, which appears to be the typical province of *language-using* conceptualisers, and which justifies talk of reasons and rationality in connection with them. Wittgenstein's comment to the effect that a dog may expect his master home, but cannot expect his master home *tomorrow*, underlines this; which is why, whereas behaviour in which X manifests practical thought relative to actions is indeed behaviour which justifies ascription to X of concepts and

[14] J. Bishop, 'More thought on thought and talk', *Mind* 89 (1980).

thus a scheme, this is not enough for our purposes; for we wish to talk in terms of *beliefs* and the awareness that some beliefs *justify* others in order to make proper sense of what is necessary to a conceptual scheme, if anything is so necessary. Only language-using conceptualisation is rich enough to admit of that kind of investigation. Accordingly it is appropriate to suggest that a conceptual scheme is to be considered focally as a language or set of intertranslatable languages, and to say that certain animals possess conceptual schemes is to say they enjoy, more or less rudimentarily, a form of conceptual experience understandable as such by derivation from our understanding of conceptual experience in the focal case. This, I think, is intuitively the appropriate way to mark the continuities and differences between animal (*qua* non-language using) and human (*qua* language-using) experience; and it affords a criterion of identity for conceptual schemes, derived from a view of them as sets of intertranslatable languages or what can be understood as conceptual experience by means of them.

It follows from this and the sense-condition on use of 'conceptual scheme' that if there is Martian or divine experience, it would have to be organised in a way recognisable to us *as* a form of organisation of experience to count as such. For all that this appears, in one sense, to be a trivial and unsatisfying consequence of restricting our grasp on what a conceptual scheme can be – and a radically anthropocentric grasp to boot – it follows ineluctably from the principle that what is possible is what makes sense. In any case, as will be seen, there are yet further good reasons for holding this parsimonious view. These will become apparent in course of discussing in more detail the issues of the nature of conceptual schemes and relativism, to which, after this detour, I now turn.

So far, conceptual schemes have been characterised as forms of organisation of experience, using this locution to capture what is intended by talk of 'points of view' or 'systems of categories that give form to the data of sense'. Despite the generality of such a characterisation, it has its usefulness. In so far as they are schemes, conceptual schemes are at least in part structured, there being relations of dependence and consequence among the beliefs in the scheme, beliefs being construed as concepts to which are attached what Korner calls 'epistemic pro- and con-attitudes'.[15] This being so, it is natural to think of the structure as having upper and lower regions, as it were, varying from more to less theoretical respectively. This would account for the fact that subscribers to the same scheme can disagree over such issues as say, God's existence, or almost any philosophical issue, without rendering the scheme as a whole incoherent. Such conceptual oppositions are comfortably comprehended within a single scheme owing to the latitude which it affords its subscribers, by the empirical underdetermination of their more general theories, to find justification for superstructurally diverse points of view on theoretical matters, that is, the general beliefs (including science) and values of their community. But, as it is my concern to argue, this latitude diminishes as one descends from the richly flourishing superstructure of the scheme to its more basic empirical substructure, where the sensefulness of concepts accrues from the more determinate empirical conditions of their applicability. It is at this level that transcendental beliefs are to be found.

Certain forms of relativism are premissed on a denial of a hierarchical model of this kind, at one extreme insisting on complete failure of translatability between schemes, or even between different historical stages of a single scheme, on the grounds that there is always a high degree of theory infecting basic empirical beliefs and observation. This is a point which merits full treatment, and I shall give it shortly. The point I am urging in contrast is that there is no *prima facie* reason, even conceding theory-ladenness of empirical concepts and observationality, to deny that schemes may differ considerably in respect of their theoretical superstructure, but hardly at all in respect of their basic empirical characteristics. This allows for the features just noted without conceding to radical relativism. Certain heuristic considerations are relevant here; Australian aboriginals are said to speak of the sun as a golden cockatoo, which flies through a geocentric universe at regularly interrupted intervals. It is neither here nor there whether they hold that the sun *is* a golden cockatoo, literally, or whether talking of the sun like this is a gloss after the fashion of the Greek myth, in which the sun is Apollo's fiery chariot. What is crucial is that *that thing*, bright and glowing and

[15] S. Korner, unpublished MS.

regularly traversing the sky westwards, is the common and identifiable topic of the discourse. A relativist might deny commensurability here, not only as between the golden cockatoo and fiery chariot views, on the one hand, and our own literal 'the sun = a burning mixture of hydrogen (81.8 per cent) and helium (18.2 per cent)' on the other hand, but between the cockatoo and chariot views themselves; and he might argue that whereas we take our characterisation of the sun – that is, of what the sun *is* – as literal, it is not even clear whether it is appropriate to talk of the aboriginal and Greek characterisations in terms of literalness or otherwise. But these cavils are undermined by the reflection just given; what the dispute is about is *that thing*, that glowing, etc., identifiable and recognisable item. Thus whether or not, to vary the example, by 'gavagai' Quine's natives mean 'rabbit' or something like 'temporal slices of rabbithood', it remains that the topic of discourse is not the mountains in the distance or that tree there, but gavagai (in some sense =) rabbit. These considerations provide a platform on which to construct the mechanism for defeating relativism of the problematic sort, as will emerge.

Given a hierarchical model of the sort sketched, what is evidently correct about relativism can be conceded without qualms. The distinction between 'moral' or 'cultural' relativism on the one hand and 'cognitive' relativism on the other becomes of use here. That there are differences between the conceptual schemes of different cultures and between phases of the history of the same culture is hardly deniable. For example, Navaho Indians are said to discriminate between two shades of black but not between blue and green, which affords a case of cultural or synchronic relativity when contrasted with our own colour classifications; and the concept of courtly or romantic love is said to date only from medieval times, and to have been lacking in Western culture beforehand, which affords a case of historical or diachronic relativity within a tradition. But these sorts of considerations are wholly unproblematic from the point of view of the purposes here, for they are not at issue; indeed, precisely because we are able to recognise that these differences exist and are able to specify them, we are entitled to conclude that there is enough in common to the cultures and historical phases in question to render them mutually accessible. Such relativism provides support for, rather than against, the thesis that conceptual schemes are not in the end very different. Even when a language contains expressions which our own does not, all that follows is that there is no '*ready* availability of a single term or a well-tailored idiom' for translation of the term,[16] not that the term is untranslatable and therefore indicative of radical conceptual relativity. Good examples are Nabokov's 'poshlost', quoted by Black, and the Eskimo's thirty-plus terms for snow. The former can be rendered as 'complacent self-satisfaction with vulgar or banal values', and the latter have renderings into English as 'wet snow', 'dry snow', 'new snow', 'old snow', 'crisp snow', 'hard snow', and so on for all thirty and more. Differences in outlook and differences in linguistic resources, so far from sealing off one scheme from another, are recognisable *as* differences only because the schemes are mutually accessible – which is to say, because translation is possible.

It is however just this latter point which has been denied by philosophical proponents of relativism, on the following grounds. The appearance of accessibility is misleading, they argue, because far from gaining entry to the aliens' conceptual scheme we have merely reinterpreted it in a systematic way into the terms of our own scheme; and this is the best we can ever hope to do, because translation is not possible above a certain highly indeterminate level. By failure of translation such relativists do not mean the empirically false thesis that no language can be rendered into another, but the philosophical thesis that (to employ Quine's terms) synonymy relations cannot be established above the level of stimulus-meanings of sentences, these being native speakers' patterns of assent and dissent to them; and therefore although we might come to use a term of a foreign language in the correct assent-dissent pattern, we can never be quite sure which of alternative translations of the term exhaustively captures its sense, for its stimulus-conditions under-determine what precise construction is to be placed upon it. Accordingly 'gavagai' might mean 'rabbit', or 'temporal slices of rabbithood', and so on, without our being able to reduce the indeterminacy.[17]

Underlying Quine's thesis of the indeterminacy of translation, and its yet more extreme variants like Feyerband's views on meaning

[16] M. Black, *Language and Philosophy*, Ithaca 1949, p. 32.
[17] Cf. Quine, *Word and Object*, ch. 2 passim.

variance,[18] is the problem about theory-ladenness of observation. If all discourse is theoretical, there is no neutral point to step upon from which subscribers to one scheme can carry out comparisons with an alien scheme. If the problem of translation proves to be intractable, it follows that relativism is true; and Quine's view, that a difference of language marks a difference of ontology, is substantiated. Accordingly the issue of theory-ladenness and its consequences for translation need to be carefully considered.

What the thesis of theory-ladenness comes down to is the denial, by its proponents, of any distinction between theoretical and observational terms. The consequence of the Vienna Circle debate on whether there can be an observation language, *protokolsätze*, or some form of theory-neutral description of experience, was that there can be no such thing, owing among other things to the fact that the notion of observationality is itself theoretical, forming part of a theory of reductive analysis; so there is no way out, on either count of whether (a) there can be a neutral observation language into which different theoretical languages can be translated for comparison, or (b) whether certain sets of one kind of theoretical statements (for instance, about physical objects) could be reduced to observational statements (for instance, about sense-data); for the distinction required to license such translations trades upon the possibility of there being formal criteria of synonymy by means of which the translation in such reductive exercises can be effected. And this is what is denied; Quine holds that there can be no such formal criteria for synonymy, because any such criteria would be constructable only by means of reference to our knowledge of what things in the world the terms in question apply to, and therefore cannot be independent of our theories about the world. Accordingly, because the synonymy relations will themselves be theory-infected, appeal to them in reduction vitiates the reductive enterprise. The truth of the claim that there can be no observation term-theoretical term distinction rests therefore on the denial of the possibility of synonomy. It is on the basis of this latter, as noted, that it is then denied that the meaning of an expression in a given natural language can be stated in another natural language, and that therefore, because the conceptual scheme is the language, failure of translation

[18] Cf. P. Feyerabend, *Against Method*, London 1978, passim.

amounts to radical relativism. Feyerabend has taken this position further by claiming that because, within a single scheme, all the concepts employed are theoretical, shifts in theory constitute conceptual change and therefore change in meaning; for example, inventing finer ways of calibrating temperature results, in Feyerabend's view, in change in the meaning of 'temperature'.

The difficulties raised by these relativist arguments may appear the more intractable from the point of view of my purposes here owing to the fact that they seem to be a natural corollary of antirealism with respect to language, and the question arises therefore whether I am forced to concede to relativist arguments on this ground. Feyerabend's thermometers afford a case in point. If the sense of a term is fixed by its conditions of assertion, evidently changes in these latter – as with finer calibrations of temperature – constitute changes of sense, and this is what Feyerabend means (or at least must mean) by a 'change of meaning'. However, this is only an apparent complication; it rests upon two mistakes to the effect that (a) the sense of a term is grasped only through possession or mastery of such facts as would *inductively* justify application of the term, so that changes in the nature of such facts involve a change of sense, because these facts constitute the term's assertion conditions, and (b) that any such change involves change of reference too. This latter part of the mistake makes illegitimate use of something right, namely that sense provides the route for reference for terms picking out abstract objects like temperature. The mistakes here are easily spotted. It is evident that being able to understand what improving our understanding of some phenomenon consists in, demands *continuity* of reference to the phenomenon, to ensure that modifications in our concept of it are intelligible – which is to say that improving, extending, or refining our understanding of something x cannot entail that *ipso facto* we cease to mean x but y instead, for then we should not have been improving or extending our grasp of x at all. An alternative example may help to clarify the point; electrons for Bohr and electrons for contemporary physicists are, as we say 'two different things', and yet understanding the recent history of particle physics demands an important minimum of continuity of reference for the term 'electron', and therefore some degree of overlap of sense; otherwise it would not be possible to talk of a change or improvement in our understanding of electrons. This ties in with the earlier part of the mistake; for to know that it is a finer way of calibrating *temperature* which has been found, the sense of 'temperature' canot have changed, and therefore cannot turn solely upon the various procedures by which temperature is measured; rather, talk of temperature is appropriate when what is at issue is, independently of the alternative ways we measure it, simply the degree of intensity of sensible heat of a body or the air. It would be absurd, and yet a direct consequence of Feyerabend's views, to hold that if I say 'it was 21° Centigrade, 69.8° Fahrenheit, or 16.8° Réaumur yesterday', I am talking about three different things. If someone came up with a new temperature scale based on letters of the alphabet, and a new kind of thermometer, and presented it to me with the request to say what the instrument measured, my failure to tell him would mean neither that I misunderstood 'temperature' (and certainly not because the term had 'changed its meaning' owing to the innovations present), nor that what a mercury thermometer measures in Fahrenheit units is different from what the new alphabetical thermometer measures. Again, that the new thermometer measures temperature is something we grasp independently of any particular technical knowledge of how temperature is measured; the sense of the term is fixed in quite general ways involving an ability to perceive sensible differences in heat – 'hotter' and 'colder' form the scale which counts, and that must be invariant with respect to sophisticated means of dealing with temperature; they are, so to say, the appearances which the sophistications must save. Accordingly, Feyerabend's mistake is to identify inductive instrumental facts and assertibility conditions, which it was noted above will not do (see Chapter 2 above), and incorrectly takes changes in such facts to entail directly correspondent changes in reference, which, if he is right, would so far dislocate our conceptual scheme as to make the notion of conceptual change itself meaningless.

It is at this point that Davidson's views on conceptual schemes become of interest, because they afford a means of eliminating much of the metaphorical slack in the notion, at the same time giving purchase against the relativism just outlined.[19] It was mentioned

[19] For further and different treatment of the views about to be discussed

above that relativism is paradoxical, because in insisting on the differences between schemes it trades upon a presupposition to the effect that the differences can be recognised as such. If the idea of differences between schemes makes sense, then it does so on the grounds of their mutual accessibility or, as Davidson puts it, on the ground that there is a 'common coordinate system' on which to plot the differences; yet 'the existence of a common system of beliefs belies the claim of dramatic incomparability'.[20] On the basis of this observation Davidson sets out to show what would count as setting bounds to conceptual contrasts, by way of an investigation of what middle ground a relativist could reasonably occupy between the paradoxical extreme relativism of Feyerabend's kind, and the modest relativism of the sort earlier characterised as unproblematic; for if the relativist is to succeed in his claim against the idea that conceptual schemes are similar in their fundamental respects, his arguments will have somehow to lie there.

It is worth repeating here the point about the identification of conceptual schemes with languages or intertranslatable sets of them, for Davidson agrees with this and makes use of it. If the relation between schemes and languages is taken to be that if schemes differ then so do languages, then users of different languages can be said to share the same scheme provided the languages are intertranslatable; and this furnishes a way, as noted, of focussing on criteria of identity for conceptual schemes, viz. by studying the criteria of translation between the languages embodying them. If it were not the case that schemes and languages are one, the vexing matter of having *two* organising frameworks would arise, and with it the question, as Davidson puts it, of 'Who is to be master?' (ibid.). Accordingly the issue comes down, for the relativist, to showing that people who speak languages which fail of intertranslatability have schemes different from each other. Such would be the case when no significant range of sentences in L_1 could be translated into L_2. The aim of an argument against relativism is to show that the notion of complete failure of intertranslatability does not make sense, and this is what

here see M. McGinn, 'The third dogma of empiricism', *Proceedings of the Aristotelian Society* (1981), and W.V.O. Quine, *Theories and Things*, Cambridge, Mass. 1981, pp. 38-42.

[20] Davidson, op. cit., p. 6.

Davidson attempts to do (p. 7).

Davidson states and then argues for this very tempting line: that if a form of activity cannot be interpreted as language by means of our language, then that activity is not speech activity. At first glance it would appear that Davidson has made a simple mistake, namely that of taking 'translatability into a familiar language' to be the criterion of languagehood; but his supporting argument shows that this may not be a mistake at all, chiefly because there is a very close relation between the possession of language and the possession of intentional concepts, the relation being that language-use demands possession of 'a multitude of finely discriminated intentions and beliefs' (p. 8), which it would be difficult to attribute to a putative speaker unless we could render his speech. Accordingly, only if we are in a position to recognise the manifestation of intentions and beliefs in a form of activity which we are inclined to think is language, can we say that it *is* language. This is a point with which Davidson makes some play in setting up a version of the notion of 'radical interpretation' (cf. pp. 17ff.). But that comes later in the story. The present problem is to understand the idea, if it can be understood, of incommensurable differences between schemes, and Davidson's treatment of this issue.

There are two kinds of metaphor for the kind of differences between schemes in question. In Strawson's view 'it is possible to imagine kinds of world very different from the world as we know it' (Strawson, p. 15), and Kuhn holds that scientists operating with different paradigms live in 'different worlds'.[21] The talk of 'different worlds' here is evidently metaphorical, intended to capture differences in interpretation or conceptualisation of a single universe; but the metaphors are themselves very different. In Davidson's view, what Strawson means is that by using our own language and redistributing truth-values across it systematically, we arrive at a 'different world'; the basic scheme and the descriptive resources remain fixed (Davidson, p. 9). By contrast, Kuhn's model is of a single world seen from different standpoints, with observers at each employing incommensurable systems of concepts. Strawson's view, although Davidson does not remark this, is not problematic because it makes the possible variant worlds parasitic upon our own for their

[21] T. Kuhn, *The Structure of Scientific Revolutions*, Chicago 1962; cf. ch. 10, esp. pp. 110, 117, 119.

intelligibility, and this fact provides purchase against any view to the effect that there are *imaginable* schemes different from our own; for arriving at them by tinkering with our own scheme bespeaks no genuine difference of scheme but only ingenuity in stretching the grounds of intelligibility afforded by the scheme we have. In contrast, Kuhn's view is genuinely relativist; as Davidson points out, whereas Strawson's metaphor evinces a dualism, within language, of concept and content (different worlds are described using one scheme, in the sense of a language whose words retain their meanings; so that the systematic redistribution of truth-values falls only over synthetic, and not analytic, sentences), Kuhn's metaphor trades on a different dualism, one of scheme as a whole, that is, language, and uninterpreted content. Kuhn's notion is the Quinean one that if the analytic-synthetic distinction is given up, with it goes the notion that we can distinguish between theory and language, with the result that, as witness Feyerabend's views, theoretical change (or difference) means semantic change (or difference). But in Davidson's view, change of terminology is not evidence for change of outlook – 'all that is being reiterated here is that, banally, truth of sentences is relative to (among other things) the language they belong to' (pp. 10-110) – from which he takes it to follow that rejecting the analytic-synthetic distinction does not by itself make relativism of Kuhn's type intelligible. So far, then, Davidson's point is that the Quinean rejection of the 'two dogmas' of empiricism – reductionism and the analytic-synthetic distinction – does not make such relativism intelligible, although it is taken by such as Kuhn and Feyerabend to lead directly to it. What *does* appear to support such relativism is the scheme-content dualism Kuhn also relies upon. Davidson takes it that the idea of empirical content is to be explained by reference to what is variously described in the literature as 'the facts, the world, experience, sensation, the totality of sensory irritations, or something similar' (p. 11), and it is here that he mounts his attack: 'I want to urge that this second dualism of scheme and content, of organising system and something waiting to be organised, cannot be made intelligible and defensible. It is itself a dogma of empiricism, the third dogma. The third, and perhaps the last, for if we give it up it is not clear that there is anything distinctive left to call empiricism' (ibid.).

The scheme-content dualism can be put in a variety of ways, but rests basically on the idea that something is a conceptual scheme or language if it stands in a certain relation over against what is given in or constitutes experience; thus the relation might be 'predicting, organising, facing or fitting' something like, respectively 'experience, reality, or sensory promptings' (p. 13). It is a major difficulty, on Davidson's view, to make sense of the relation in question and its relata. In general there are two main identifiable groups of relations; on the one hand, relations of organising or systematising or 'dividing up' (the stream of experience), and, on the other hand, predicting, accounting for, or 'facing' (the tribunal of experience). For the first group the objective relatum is typically taken to be reality, that is, the universe, the world, or nature; and for the second it is typically experience, variously described as the passing show, surface irritations, sense-data, the given.[22] Davidson holds that neither group of metaphors will permit a relativist construction, and gives these reasons.

Metaphors of organisation or systematisation turn on an ontological presupposition to the effect that the world contains a plurality of things, for, as Davidson puts it, you can organise the contents of a closet but not the closet itself (ibid.). On a relativist view, failure of translation would come down, in terms of this metaphor, to there being predicates in L_1 whose extensions are not matched by predicates in L_2, or to which there are not even partially correlative predicates in L_2. But being able to establish a point like this demands access to one language from the other, because breakdowns in translation can be spotted only against a background of general success in translation. Because this must be so, Davidson concludes that the metaphor will not support relativism. The relativist, it will be remembered, in attempting to make sense of failure of translation, is in need of a criterion for languagehood which neither depends on nor entails the translatability of an alien language into a familiar idiom. Davidson's point is that no such criterion is available on the basis of 'the image of organising the closet of nature'. Neither will it do, on his view, to talk in the same way of the organisation of *experience*, because much the same difficulties recur. Once again, 'organisation' makes sense only with

[22] Ibid., p. 14. Either group of objective relata can be associated with either group of relations, on Davidson's view; but these are the typical pairings.

respect to a plural ontology, and even if the ontology is one of events rather than things 'we would have to individuate according to familiar principles' (p. 15). But talk of experiences, or sensory irritation, and the like, involves an added difficulty, which Davidson formulates in the question 'how could something count as a language that organised only experiences; for surely knives and forks, railroads and mountains, need organising too?'[23]

The other group of metaphors – 'fitting' and 'facing' – involves a somewhat different set of problems, because the change from talk of organisation to talk of fitting involves a change from the referential apparatus of language – quantifiers, variables, singular terms, and predicates – to whole sentences. The idea of language fitting experience is not that the sole subject matter of language is surface irritations (that is, that talk of objects is to be analysed as talk of sense-data), but that sensory experience provides *all* the evidence for acceptance of sentences, some of which may be whole theories; the point being 'that for a theory to fit or face up to the totality of possible sensory evidence is for that theory to be true' (pp. 15-16). Davidson's objection to this is that talk of fitting the totality of experience, or 'fitting the facts' or 'being true to the facts', 'adds nothing to the simple concept of being true' (p. 16). Accordingly the relativist criterion for languagehood becomes: 'largely true but not translatable.' The question whether this is a workable criterion depends upon whether the notion of truth in a language can be understood independently of the notion of translation. The answer is 'no'; for it is only by imputing to aliens an attitude of 'holding true' with respect to their assertions that we can even begin to interpret their behaviour *as* speech behaviour, and thus to attribute beliefs and intentions to them; and so the idea of having a grasp of truth in a language involves a breach in the putative seals between the languages at issue, and provides means for a 'going method' of translation, which Davidson calls 'radical interpretation' (p. 18). If all that is known to us is which sentences of an alien tongue a speaker of it holds true, then because interpreting his speech involves

[23] Ibid. I let this pass in my critical comments below because, on the basis of the argument in Chapter 2 above regarding essential reference to objects, this consideration, on a construal derived from that argument, suggests something correct.

knowing or assuming a great deal about his beliefs, we assume as a matter of course *and* of necessity (doing so is 'not at option') a general agreement on beliefs between ourselves and him, and (a principle of charity) to maximise agreement we give him the benefit of the doubt to the effect that he is right most of the time in his holdings-true (p. 19). That is, being able to recognise the alien language as a language demands that we assume that we share a community of beliefs with the speakers of that language. 'If we can produce a theory that reconciles charity and the formal conditions for a theory, we have done all that could be done to ensure communication' (ibid.).' Differences become more meaningful the fewer of them there are; such differences thus turn out to be differences of opinion rather than conceptualisation, and therefore, Davidson concludes, there is no content to the idea of 'conceptual relativism'. He takes this to mean that the very idea of 'conceptual schemes' itself is empty, suggesting as it does diversity and 'points of view'. Because, in the end, there is no real conceptual diversity but only difference of opinion, the locution itself might as well be 'scrapped' (p. 20).

There is much of use in these views, not least in the respects in which they are arguably wrong. Their crucial point is that nothing could count as a language unless it were recognisable as such to us, and that differences in outlook or opinion, in order to be recognised as differences, would have to occur against a wide background of mutual comprehensibility and a wide range of shared beliefs and assumptions. This seems to me right, and promises to be decisive against conceptual relativism. But if the crucial point is that language must be recognisable as such to be such, a question arises about what, precisely, would have to be recognised, and how; on these points Davidson is vague. In particular, the 'going method' of radical interpretation appears to be insufficiently strong to provide the required depth of access to the belief-structure which the alien language represents, for, in connection with the ordinary empirical beliefs to which the aliens will occasionally commit themselves in their discourse, being clear about their nature is necessary to getting clear about the ontology presupposed to them. Because grasping the essentials of the scheme's ontology could not wait upon a command at large of the language – the problem, after all, is to recognise the language *as* a language *to begin with* – there must be something about the details of the languagehood criterion such that applying it, or being able to apply it, somehow reveals the relevant ontological features.

Schematically: a language is a conceptual scheme. In recognising the language (conceptual scheme) as a language, we recognise the presence of a certain range of beliefs, specifically empirical beliefs. Evidently what these beliefs are is the important issue, and what features or devices of the language they reveal themselves in will constitute those features or devices the presence of which will enable us to recognise the language as a language. The task is to specify these.

Davidson's views turn on a choice between the metaphors of 'organisation' and 'facing' and what follows from making such a choice. As noted, he chooses the latter metaphor, predictably enough, because he shares with Quine a holistic as opposed to a 'building block' theory of language, in which evidence does not come sentence by sentence, but confronts the language as a whole.[24] On such a view the notion of reference has little part to play; if the allowable evidence for interpretation of a language L_1 is contained in a translation manual M, then all that M helps us to do is to go from sentences of L_1 to sentences of L_2, without our being able to infer anything about the nexuses between words and objects in L_1. In any case, Davidson holds that reference is an obscure notion even in connection with one's own language; certainly no M gives enlightenment on reference, for translation on his view is a syntactic notion purely, and grasping syntax does nothing to explain reference (ibid). Moreover, for the familiar reasons Davidson advances in arguing for a theory which will specify a structure by means of which an infinite number of T-sentences can be generated, no antecedent appeal to the semantic notions of reference and satisfaction can be made owing to the requirement that nothing outside the conceptual resources of a given sentence should be employed in stating its truth-conditions. Thus if we employ a Carnap-style rule[25] to the effect that a sentence consisting of a singular term *a* and a one-place predicate *F* is true if and only if the object named by *a* belongs to the class determined by *F*, then the requirement is violated. By contrast,

[24] Cf. D. Davidson, 'Reality without reference', *Dialectica* 31 (1977), p. 251.

[25] Cf. R. Carnap, *Meaning and Necessity*, Chicago 1956, p. 5.

if for any such sentence *Fa* there is a postulate to the effect that the object *a* is a member of the class determined by *F*, then this would provide a means of stating T-sentences without violating the requirement; it would be the case that to each T-sentence there is a postulate, which could only be the case if the lists of names and predicates were finite, and therefore there would be only a finite list of *Fa*-type sentences, so that nothing would stand in the way of stating the truth-conditions for such sentences straight off, the *Fa* sentences themselves serving as axioms with no appeal made to an antecedent notion of reference.[26]

The question is, given these implications of the metaphor he chooses, is Davidson's choice of metaphor correct? That is, does radical interpretation provide a way of specifying the languagehood criterion by means of which relativism is to be refuted? My suggestion is that it does not, and that in fact it is the other metaphor – 'organisation' – which provides the right way of dealing with the problem.

Davidson noted that whether the notion of 'organising' was taken as applying to the world or to experience, it makes sense only on condition that what gets organised is a plurality, and, because of this, relativism with respect to the alien scheme will not work, owing to the fact that if the alien scheme organises a plural ontology then failure in translation will be a direct function of failure in matchings between the extension of predicates in the alien and familiar tongues, which could only be grasped at all if enough of the alien scheme were accessible. It is first to be noted that this counter to relativism trades upon what, familiarly, Davidson later and elsewhere follows Quine in denying, namely referential scrutability; for grasping the allied facts that alien speakers individuate items, and delimit the extensions of predicates which apply to them, in just the way that they do, depends upon being able to grasp *what* the alien speakers pick out and count together by means of the devices which, in grasping their activity, we *ipso facto* recognise as linguistic devices for individuation and predication. A restatement of the argument reveals this clearly: if a language (scheme) organises the world or experience, then the ontology at issue is pluralist; accordingly the

[26] Cf. D. Davidson, 'The method of truth in metaphysics' in French et al. (edd.) *Contemporary Perspectives in the Philosophy of Language*, Minneapolis 1979, p. 296.

language must contain individuative devices (and thus concepts of individuals) and predicative devices (and thus concepts of properties) as does ours; for otherwise noting failure in co-exstensivity of predicates between our own and the alien language would be impossible (in the perfectly appropriate sense of 'senseless'). Accordingly, at least part of the languagehood criterion is that if anything is a language it contains devices for individuation and for ascribing properties to the individuals individuated, which devices can be recognised as such in a way exactly parallel to our understanding – which is to say, being able to use – the same linguistic features of familiar idioms. The translatability of the alien tongue will indeed rest upon this; for not even recognising assent and dissent patterns, after the Quine model, would be possible unless we recognised that (taking the simplest cases) what the assent or dissent is relative to is a claim that here or there is something x or that x is or is not something F. At the base of a model of discourse which is built upon the idea, surely right, that at its simplest communication rests upon pointing out, agreeing upon, or denying, as the case may be, such matters as these, is the notion that an x can be marked off from the rest of the perceptual field, and that something can be said about x, i.e. that some property can be ascribed to it (or denied of it), such as that it stands in a certain relation (to, say, y), or is spotted, or is of a certain kind, or is about to pounce. Evidently, a wholly uninterpreted discourse would be one just in virtue of our failure to recognise certain strings of sounds or marks as what might on the foregoing be called individuative and predicative claims, for – the reason noted – our failure in this respect would deny us purchase even on what is to count as assent or dissent. It follows that being able to recognise a language as such comes down to being able to recognise certain of its features as individuative and predicative in function.

It is important to notice at this point how taking such a view marks an advance over the Quine-Davidson line. Quine allows that for a certain range of sentences, namely 'observation sentences' falling on to the periphery of the web of language, meanings can be grasped by 'pure ostension'. Mass terms are good examples; 'water' can be learned ostensively by conditioning or induction. In contrast, terms of divided reference like 'rabbit' cannot be mastered without mastering the principles of individuation governing them, yet these cannot be mastered by ostension; therefore indeterminacy enters the picture, for if one cannot tell, in connection with 'gavagai', where one leaves off and another begins, e.g. whether 'gavagai' picks our rabbits, undetached rabbit parts, or rabbit stages, then appeal to reference is of no avail in accounting for however much of the meaning of 'gavagai' we grasp, and in consequence we have to rest content, in trying to do so, with indeterminate 'stimulus-meaning'.[27] This alone on Quine's view is what enables us to get our translation manual started. But this will not do; for, as Harrison points out, all that the stimulus-conditions for 'gavagai' tell us is that 'gavagai' is assertible when current stimulation includes a rabbit, and that native speakers never dissent when 'gavagai' is offered in the presence of one.[28] But this is to know far too little about the assertibility-conditions of 'gavagai' to permit translation of the term, for it may be, as some widely different set of circumstances might show, that 'gavagai' means something like 'creature which yields white meat', and may therefore also apply to chickens. Unless the translator had a way of focussing on what the term contrasts with in native usage, that is, on what it is for something to be '*not* gavagai', he could not render the term. Among the complexities known to a speaker about the sentences of his own language are some of the implications which use of them carries; in particular, interpreting a sentence (e.g. 'This is not red') involves knowing that it implies a certain closed field of options, having the force of 'This is (some other colour)' rather than, say, 'This is liquid' or 'This tastes pleasant' (ibid.). Unless the translator knew what remained open by a case of dissent to 'gavagai', the expression would be wholly opaque; yet to know the force of such a denial would be to know a principle of individuation for gavagais, for the simple reason that the translator would know, in knowing what was left open by denials, *ipso facto* where one gavagai left off and another began. Accordingly, for any sort of interpretation to get going, what must be known to the translator is the reference of the relevant terms. And the notion of reference here is not particularly arcane; the reference of a term is just the object which use of the term (if it is a singular term) picks out

[27] Cf. W.V.O. Quine, *Ontological Relativity and Other Essays*, New York 1961, pp. 31ff.

[28] Cf. B. Harrison, *Introduction to Philosophy of Language*, London 1979, pp. 116-17.

or individuates, or the objects which the term (if it is a general term) collects.

If it is granted that references must be perspicuous across languages for translation to be possible, it follows that the extension of at least many simple predicates, or, at any rate, the intersection of the extension of such predicates as between the languages, is determinable; for referential scrutability allows the direct enumeration of lists of objects satisfying a predicate in a way which would permit correct application (and withholdings) of a predicate in L_1 by a speaker of L_2. It follows that for some expressions paired from L_1 and L_2 there will be a semantic feature of the pairing suspiciously like our pretheoretical grasp of intralanguage synonymy; 'La plume est rouge' and 'The pen is red' is a case in point. Evidently, if such a relation obtains between sentences of different languages, it does so in a way both richer and more determinate than is allowable on Quine's view of stimulus-synonymy; and this is as it should be, for the perspicuity of reference and accessibility of predicate-extensions across languages would be expected to generate together a number of unquestionable matchings of this kind as a direct consequence. This is not (or not directly) a point about intralanguage synonymy in the sense of intersubstitutivity of terms or expressions in sentential contexts *salva veritate*; rather, holding for present purposes to the level of complete sentences of a given class, viz. sentences expressing perceptual judgments, it is a point about statement synonymy within and across languages. It will be recalled that in 'Two Dogmas' Quine attacked both the analytic-synthetic distinction and reductionism on the grounds that they are closely linked and mutually supportive, depending as they do on the possibility of extricating factual from semantic considerations of a given statement separately, which, if it were possible, would make reduction a feasible enterprise in that we could display the factual component of truth-conditions independently of the purely semantical features of sentences made true (or false) by them, and we could give an account of analytic statements as constituting a degenerate class wholly dependent for their truth-value on semantical considerations alone. Quine's attack was an attack on Positivist verificationism, to which this 'extricability thesis' was fundamental.[29] Statement

[29] Dummett calls Quine's rejection of this thesis 'the inextricability

synonymy in the Positivist view consists in the fact that because the meaning of a statement is its method of verification, any two statements with identical empirical conditions of confirmation or disconfirmation are synonymous. This demands that unique ranges of sensory events should be identifiable for individual statements which, as the case may be, verify or falsify the statements in question; and it is this in which the reductionism of the view consists and which Quine finds objectionable. His holism or 'organic' verification is opposed precisely to this 'molecular' verificationism.[30] But it is by no means clear that what Quine takes to follow from the adoption of a holistic view *does* follow, specifically in connection with indeterminacy of the level of observation statements. Here, on his view, the stimulus meanings of observation sentences, construed as the ordered pair of assents and dissents prompted by given stimuli, underdetermine the translation of such sentences from L_1 to L_2 in the way noted; but for the reason that the range of options left open by dissents must be determinate – again, as noted – this degree of indeterminacy would prevent any translation at all. Quine's notion of stimulus-meaning as it stands will not therefore do, and the added requirement that the force of dissents be available to the translator is precisely a requirement for determinacy. This has two results: it entails that sentences indeterminate in L_2 will reflect indeterminacy in L_1 in the way described by Dummett (pp. 395ff..), that is, that if a sentence of L_1 has competing renderings in L_2, then this will be because speakers of L_1 themselves attach competing interpretations to the sentence in L_1, and this feature of the sentence's ambiguity or underdetermination will be reflected in L_2; and secondly, it entails that the assertibility-conditions for unambiguous sentences of L_1 will be known to a speaker of L_2 if he can translate it, in such a way that for at least some sentences of L_1 the speaker of L_2 can recognise the assertibility-conditions for the sentence to be identical to its translation in L_2, and so stand in a relation of statement-synonymy to its L_2 translation.[31]

---

thesis'; thus the coining here. Cf. Dummett, 'The significance of Quine's indeterminacy thesis' in *Truth and Other Enigmas*, London 1979.

[30] Dummett's coinings, ibid., p. 379.

[31] It is, familiarly, an unavoidable complication that, however demarcated, sentences in a language have different degrees of theoreticity.

It is important to note how this notion of statement-synonymy unpacks. It trades upon the fact that determinacy of reference and predicate extension must be available to the translator if he is to translate at all. Thus if he knows that a term *a* in L_1 refers to all and only what the term α in L_2 refers to, and a predicate *F* introduces a particular property designated Θ in L_2, then the sentence *Fa* in L_1 is synonymous with the L_2 sentence $\Theta\alpha$. It is to be recalled that understanding (knowing how to use) a sentence involves knowing all of (a) what terms correlate with what features of a perceptual environment, (b) how to recognise such features, and (c) in what ways things can go wrong with either (a) or (b) and chiefly the latter (see Chapter 2 above). Knowing, at least implicitly, these things is to know how to use, that is, understand, the sentence. To assert as it were *across* languages, it might seem that what has to be known is extra information under (a), for example that 'plume' corefers with 'pen', 'voiture' with 'motor-car' and so on; but matters are somewhat tighter than this, for knowing (a) essentially involves knowing (b) and (c) as well; displaying mastery of a term presupposes mastery of all three conditions. Because understanding a sentence of L_1 involves the same as understanding a sentence of L_2, knowing extra information about terms (or rather, just knowing more terms) which apply to certain features in perceptual environments is to know how things must be for their use to be warranted. This strengthens the requirement of option-closure connected with negation. For it is a corollary of these conditions that one has failed in grasping the sense of an expression if one does not know what alternatives are left open by dissent to a term, for all one would know in such a case is *that* the use of the term was inappropriate, not *why* or *how*, and this violates the conditions for mastery.

This is not to say, however, that unique ranges of sensory evidence are or have to be available for the confirmation or disconfirmation of a sentence in order for it to be *assertible*, although they would be

For more rather than less theoretical sentences, underdetermination and therefore same-language indeterminacy will be greater than for more rather than less observational sentences. The first entailment speaks to the former more than to the second, and *vice versa* for the second entailment. Observational or perceptual statements are what chiefly concern me here, however, and my remarks centre upon them unless qualified; indeterminacy reaches vanishing-point with members of this class.

available on each occasion of an undefeatedly warranted use of such a sentence. What the speaker has to know is what circumstances would warrant use of the sentence; if there are such circumstances, the sentence is assertible. The conditions for understanding a sentence do not require that for every understood sentence there is an occasion on which a speaker was actually warranted in its use. A difficulty may appear to arise here: it follows, most clearly in connection with option-closure, that understanding a sentence involves understanding other sentences, or more generally a portion at least of a language. This would seem to require of a translator that he knows other sentences of L_1 before he can understand whatever sentence of L_1 is in question. Not so; in so far as he is a *translator*, he knows L_2, and the sentence of L_1 at issue can be placed in the context of what can be said in L_2 on the topic in hand. This affords an alternative means of marking the sense in which, for a language to be recognisable as a language, it must be accessible, that is, translatable into a familiar idiom.

To revert now to the main point in hand, concerning the choice of metaphor ('organising' *versus* 'facing'): it is clear why it will not do to choose the second metaphor, as Davidson does in maintaining, if not exactly then in outline, Quine's holistic approach. In essence, the objection I have urged is that on such a view, owing to the degree of indeterminacy it imputes to best translation, translation would not be possible. If translation is possible only on the grounds that the reference and predicate extensions of some expressions in the alien tongue can be determined, then choice of the first, 'organising', metaphor becomes attractive for better reasons than just that it is the one left.

A preliminary question arises as to whether Davidson's division of the groups of metaphors into two is exhaustive. Any metaphor employed in the investigation of thought and talk about the world has to provide a means, in the nature of the case, for understanding what looks to be a relation; for the phenomena which we take to be present are, on the one hand, thought and language addressed to a world, and on the other hand that world. On the pre-theoretical level it appears that the world lies 'out there' passively and impassively following its own inexorable routines, while thought and talk of it busies itself with making and remaking connections, and describing, reporting, noting and predicting them, on this basis furnishing the elements for plans of intervention in the world, which, when executed, very often have effect. What is noteworthy about the mundane uses of thought and language is the fact that they are used in great part for practical reasonings about the world. Essential to practical reasoning are data, especially of the sort which consist in knowledge of similarities and regularities in the course of things, so that there can be reasonable expectations about how things will be in future, and how alike some new state of affairs will be to other known and similar states of affairs. Drawing the phenomena into patterns of contrast, similarity and regularity in this way is most happily described by means of a metaphor of *organisation.* In fact, it is hard to see what alternative metaphor would do as well. The one adopted by Quine and Davidson has the air of a quasi-Occasionalist theory, with total theory 'facing' the world and interacting with it in highly underdetermined fashion at points on the periphery. Such a view is oddly at variance with the fact that thinkers and talkers are rude mechanics all in their hourly doings, in which doings a lump by lump empirical language is much involved.

These considerations are very general and have no more than heuristic force, but that is all that can be expected in connection with metaphors. What they suggest, however, is that the question is not whether Davidson's division of metaphors into two groups is exhaustive (it being implied that there may be further groups of metaphors available), but rather that any metaphor which does not account for the relation between thought and talk on the one hand, and the world on the other hand, in a way which focusses on the use of the former to seek and assert contrasts, similarities and regularities respecting the latter, is going to be of little value; and that the most natural figure to use, therefore, is that of organising. Now, the Davidsonian reply would be that there are at least two good reasons for rejecting or at any rate questioning preference for this metaphor over the 'facing' or some other metaphor, these being that (1) 'organising' is too general; we need to know in more detail what the relata are, and anyway (and more seriously) (2) using such a metaphor appears to trade on the scheme-content dualism which Davidson rejects as the 'third and last dogma of empiricism' and which involves the very extricability thesis Quine's attack centres upon. In short, the motive for holism is precisely the motive for rejecting a metaphor of organisation.

On the first point, it is evident from the foregoing that the possibility of an account of experience rests upon having a distinction, already noted in connection with Carnap, between what counts as subjective (for example one's perceptions) and objective (for example those accusatives of one's perceptions which, typically, we take to be the independent causes of them). Given such a distinction, the relata are the subject of experience and the items which the subject contrasts, compares, and notes connections between, usually (and certainly pretheoretically) on the assumption that they are the independent causes of his perceptions, namely objects and events involving them. The relation between them is an internal relation, and as such is specified in specifying the relata; subject, object and the nature and function of the subject's experience of objects hang together inextricably. This is a matter of the logic of describing experience, and is not a consequence of a particular ontological view; rather, whatever ontology is settled upon stands as a consequence rather than a presupposition of an account of experience. For this reason, as noted (see Chapter 2), an idealist experience has to admit of a classification into subjective and objective components; the criteria employed in drawing the distinction between them is what issues in ontology. It follows that it is a misapprehension to view the existence of a scheme-content duality as a corollary of the 'organising' metaphor at all. Dualism would be a direct corollary of a view consisting in the theses that (a) it is possible to give an account of experience in which nothing follows as to the ontological status of its accusatives, and (b) the accusatives of experience are in fact objective (in the realist sense). Such a view would meet Davidson's implicit requirements for duality, but it is evident that its implausibility makes it an unlikely candidate as a view in need of refutation. The closest any view comes to it is what Mackie calls 'linguistic phenomenalism',[32] but I seriously doubt whether espousers of that version of phenomenalism would have thought so themselves. Kuhn, as noted above, is taken to task by Davidson for holding a view which appears to trade upon a scheme-content duality of some kind, but it is precisely the point of a refutation of Kuhn's sort of relativism that the scheme so far depends on what it constitutes as its content, and that (empirical) content is so far

[32] J.L. Mackie, 'What's really wrong with phenomenalism?' *Proceedings of the British Academy*, 55 (1968), pp. 14-16.

invariant between schemes, that relativism fails; 'points of view' differ by opinions and not by mutually sealed-off conceptualisations of experience, as Davidson himself argues. The metaphor of 'organisation', in other words, of its nature implies that the scheme *is* the content as organised, not, in any version of the metaphor's employment, something independent of or other than the content. Yet it does not follow from this that it is senseless to talk of the *relation* between thought and talk, on the one hand, and their objects, on the other, for the reason that the mere assertion of their interdependence tells us nothing about the direction or nature of their interdependence, which is what, crucially, we wish to know. On the foregoing arguments, the relation is to be correctly described as this: thought and talk presuppose a belief in the existence of objects as a necessary condition of their intelligibility or coherence.

At the same time, admitting the strength of the inextricability thesis impels us neither to accept the degree of holism demanded by Quine nor therefore the relativism which follows from it, as argued in the preceding paragraphs. The result is that a line is steered between relativism and realism in a way which leaves room for the overall claim being defended here: that certain transcendental beliefs (in particular the assumption of objects) is necessary to the coherence of conceptual experience (the sensefulness of language), and that anything recognisable as such depends upon the same set of transcendental beliefs.

It seems to me of interest that whereas, upon first examination of the issues, it appears that realism and antirelativism, on the one hand, and antirealism and relativism, on the other, pair naturally, none the less a closer scrutiny reveals that one can adopt antirealism as the most plausible account of at least this area of language, with all that follows for the correlative epistemological issue of the justification of our ordinary beliefs about the world, and yet avoid relativism. This cuts across *prima facie* boundaries in a way which seems to me interestingly foreshadowed by Kant.

The sceptic has appeared in this chapter in the guise of relativist, doubting that use of the notion of a conceptual scheme will permit the settling of his doubts. It remains now to discuss the issue of transcendental arguments, and to this I turn.

CHAPTER FOUR

Transcendental Arguments

Two transcendental arguments – or at any rate two major transcendental arguments – have appeared in the preceding two chapters, one in each. The transcendental argument in Chapter 2 sought to establish that no sense can be made of how perceptual discourse works unless that discourse is seen to presuppose a belief, held by discoursers, to the effect that their experience and talk ranges over a domain of perception-independent particulars; which was put by saying that our thought and talk is in general justified by its inherence in a conceptual scheme which is a scheme of spatio-temporal particulars. The transcendental argument in Chapter 3 sought to establish that there is only one conceptual scheme. If both arguments work, then the conjunction of their conclusions shows that the sceptical challenge, concerning what justification we have for believing that there are objects, is answered by showing that it is wholly idle to doubt that there are objects. To show that scepticism on this head is idle is to defeat scepticism. All that remains to complete this antisceptical project is to defend the form of argument – transcendental argument – used in Chapters 2 and 3 to that end.

It is important to recall that the arguments in Chapters 2 and 3 were designed to spell out and make more explicit the intuition which underlies Hume's naturalism and Wittgenstein's views in *On Certainty*, namely that scepticism is idle because we cannot help but believe in the existence of objects; that, in other words, this belief is so fundamental that it is senseless or futile to call it into question. My purpose here has been to give a fuller account of how and why this is so. In what now follows, I discuss and defend the method employed in doing so.

The transcendental argument in Chapter 3 is an argument for the uniqueness of our conceptual scheme. Its steps are clear; I revert to it below. The transcendental argument in Chapter 2 is more complex and diffuse, and is as it stands enthymematic. I shall restate it schematically and discuss it below. First, however, it is necessary to consider the questions of transcendental arguments in general. I begin by considering the nature of transcendental arguments, expounding two interpretations of them, and defending one; of the two interpretations, one is a stronger but implausible construal, the other a weaker but plausible construal which needs antirelativist arguments as a supplement (and which Chapter 3 supplied.) I then go on to display the contrast between the two interpretations of transcendental arguments by applying the lessons learned in the earlier part of this chapter in a more detailed way to particular transcendental arguments. Finally, armed with the results of the preceding discussion, I restate the transcendental argument of Chapter 2 and comment on some important features and consequences of it.

Transcendental arguments (henceforth TAs for brevity) were brought into philosophical prominence by the work of Kant, and it is appropriate to look at their Kantian provenance when setting out to try to determine what they are and what, if anything, we can hope to achieve by their use. Nevertheless, there are good reasons for not getting enmeshed in Kantian exegesis, which is the province of a large specialist industry. Industries of this sort arise because the philosophical views upon which they focus are at once important and obscure. Bennett puts the matter well by saying, of one especially relevant part of the first *Critique*, namely the Transcendental Deduction, that it is a 'desperately ill-written jungle' and a 'botch' which is nevertheless far from being a 'negligible botch'.[1] The dangers which arise from paying too little attention to the provenance of a philosophical issue are obvious, but those arising from paying too *much* are less so; they include, chiefly, becoming too embroiled in exegetical labours to see the wood for the trees. In what follows, accordingly, I shall discuss Kant's notion of TAs only in so far as it is relevant to what I take to be an otherwise wholly contemporary debate.[2]

[1] J. Bennett, *Kant's Analytic*, London 1966, p. 100.

[2] TAs have been quite widely discussed since Strawson's use of them in *Individuals* and *Bounds of Sense*; cf. e.g. B. Stroud, 'Transcendental

First, then, to consider Kant's notion of a TA. It is instructive to look at this by way of one *mistaken* interpretation of Kant's views, an interpretation owing to Hintikka.[3] Hintikka argues that what counted as 'transcendental' for Kant was the synthetic knowledge acquired a priori by 'the active aspect of our "cognitive faculty" ', in the sense that 'transcendental knowledge' is to be thought of as a kind of 'maker's knowledge produced after a plan of reason's own'. The textual support cited by Hintikka is the often-quoted sentence at A11=B25: 'I entitle *transcendental* all knowledge which is occupied not so much with objects as with the mode of our knowledge of objects insofar as this mode of knowledge is to be possible a priori', together with what Kant says in the preface to the second edition (Bxviii): '... we can know a priori of things only what we ourselves put into them.' Hintikka further concludes that recent TAs are spurious because unKantian. He says that Strawson was not entitled to call his argument to the primacy of material bodies in *Individuals* a *transcendental* argument, because the special role accorded to bodies by Strawson 'has nothing to do with any constructive activity of our "faculty to knowledge" ', and because Strawson's scheme of reidentification for material particulars is 'not produced by reason after a plan of its own'.

Hintikka's mistake does not concern his reading of 'transcendental', but his reading of Kant's idea of a 'mode of knowledge'. Evidently interpreting this to signify a mode of *acquisition* of a special kind of knowledge – namely, synthetic a priori knowledge – Hintikka takes a TA to be an argument showing how such acquisition is

---

arguments', *Journal of Philosophy* 65 (1968) and 'Transcendental arguments and "epistemological naturalism" ', *Philosophical Studies* 31 (1977); A. Phillips Griffiths & J.J. Macintosh, 'Transcendental arguments' (symposium), *Proceedings of the Aristotelian Society* supp. 43 (1969); W.A. Berriman, 'Strawson's *Individuals* as descriptive metaphysics', *Australian Journal of Philosophy* 45 (1967); T.E. Wilkerson, 'Transcendental arguments', *Philosophical Quarterly* 20 (1970); R. Harrison, 'Strawson on outer objects', *Philosophical Quarterly* 20 (1970); J. Rosenberg, 'Transcendental arguments revisited', *Journal of Philosophy* 25 (1975), and 'Reply to Stroud', *Philosophical Studies* 31 (1977); R.C.S. Walker, *Kant*, London 1979; S. Korner, 'The impossibility of transcendental deductions', *Monist* 51 (1967); E. Schaper, 'Arguing transcendentally', *Kant-Studien* 63 (1972); J. Hintikka, 'Transcendental arguments genuine and spurious', *Nous* 6 (1972); etc.

[3] J. Hintikka, op. cit., pp. 274-5ff.

effected.[4] He thus appears to get the wrong end of the stick altogether; for it is reasonably clear that what Kant intended was that transcendental knowledge should be thought of as what, as it is put in Muller's translation (p. 9), 'is occupied not so much with objects, as with our a priori concepts of objects'. Accordingly it becomes reasonably clear why Kant selected the metaphor of a legal deduction, an establishing of right or justification, to characterise the argument to those concepts and principles which we know a priori (A84=B116). Kant says: 'The explanation of the manner in which concepts can thus relate a priori to objects I entitle their transcendental deduction', and at the same point he explicitly distinguishes this proceeding from empirical deduction, which concerns not the legitimacy but the mere 'mode of *origination*' of concepts acquired a posteriori (A85=B117, my italics). How we proceed with respect to these latter cannot provide a model for how we are to settle the *quid juris* issue of the role played by a priori concepts in making experience *itself* possible (A95-B126). Here the task is to provide a vindication of title, not to show where the concepts come from. The sense in which part of what Hintikka says is right, viz. that the a priori concepts play a role in the constitution of the objective world of appearances, therefore shows the sense in which he is wrong; for in constituting reality in this sense, the concepts at issue are evidently too fundamental to admit of the kind of investigation into their 'certificates of birth', as Kant puts it, to which empirical concepts are amenable (A86-B119).

Kant's notion of a TA, therefore, is that of an argument designed to show the role played by certain a priori concepts in our knowledge of the phenomenal world. The role he claims they play is that of making experience possible. Recasting this in programmatic terms, Kant's TAs, of which there are a number throughout the first *Critique*, are demonstrations of the conditions for the possibility of experience. It is a slightly Pickwickian sense therefore in which Kant talks of the *right* we have to employ these concepts, because it turns out that, owing to their being what makes experience possible, we are not so much justified in using them as bound to use them.

[4] The misunderstanding, I think, may turn on something suggested by Kemp Smith's translation in which occurs 'mode of knowledge' rather than (as suggested by Muller) 'manner of knowing'. The original German is unenlightening on this point, licensing both.

It is this aspect of the matter which has variously elicited interest or indignation among subsequent philosophers, and in two related ways. One of these concerns finding out whether Kant's efforts will do in their own right, and if not (the consensus is that they will not) to tinker with them until they *will* do. The other is to take seriously the spirit, but not so much the detail, of Kant's enterprise, and attempt to find out what if any concepts are indispensably presupposed to our making judgments or to our thinking of the world as a system of spatio-temporal particulars. This is what Ross Harrison and Strawson, among others, have done. It is to the question of TAs in this more programmatic sense that the following is addressed.

Kant's central question was about the possibility of synthetic a priori knowledge. Answers to this question rest upon answers to a more inclusive question: the question whether there are conditions necessarily presupposed to coherent and intelligible experience in general. In just the same way as contemporary users of TAs, Kant is reasoning transcendentally, in the programmatic sense at issue, when he sets out to show that any description of experience trades upon certain distinctions and concepts, to which essential reference must be made if such a description is to be possible. In arguing for the categories, and for space and time as the pure forms of sensibility, Kant is arguing that there can be experience only under certain conditions; and this is the point of interest. Purely and simply from the standpoint of the *form* of this kind of reasoning, Kant's procedure is to argue that there must be something *Y* if there is something *X* of which *Y* is a necessary condition. In the crudest outline, then, this kind of procedure or enterprise – the search for key necessary conditions – is what might be called the 'transcendental strategy'.

In these very general terms, transcendental-style reasonings are by no means unique to the first *Critique*, nor indeed do all of them model themselves upon what is to be found in that source. Wittgenstein in the *Philosophical Investigations* and *On Certainty* argues transcendentally about the impossibility of private languages and the possibility of knowledge, respectively, and Austin's earlier solution to certain problems bedevilling the correspondence theory of truth – that is, his distinction between demonstrative and descriptive conventions – is as it were a proto-transcendentally argued point in the sense that it sets out to show that some such distinction is required for a certain other concept to have application. A somewhat stronger and more noticeably 'proto-transcendental' example of Austinian (and indeed Rylean) use of this style of reasoning is afforded by the antisceptical use of polar-concept arguments. It turns out, in short, that the method of showing that, if a given concept *x* has application then there is some other thing, or at least some other applicable concept, *y*, owing to *y*'s being a necessary condition for the applicability of *x*, is after all a quite commonplace and familiar proceeding.

None the less there is a marked difference between reasonings of these familiar sorts and the weightier, more ambitious TAs proper which are to be found in the first *Critique* or in Strawson or Harrison. One way to mark the distinction is to point to the fact that the weaker and more local proceedings just sketched share with weightier TAs no more than a certain methodological form, as this is to be described in the general terms given; namely, showing what is a necessary condition for the applicability of some concept or range of concepts. On the whole, not only is there nothing particularly unfamiliar about reasonings with this kind of aim, there is also a large risk, owing to their parochiality, of their not being very useful or very interesting. Thus, for example, the claim that we can have a concept of illusion only if we can distinguish between illusory and veridical experience neither gets us far nor tells us much; yet, on the broad characterisation given, to reason like this is to reason rather as Kant was doing. What marks off weightier TAs from such reasonings is therefore something extra. The something extra is that TAs proper are not concerned with the conditions under which particular conceptual polarities like 'illusory-veridical' or 'being right–being wrong' have application, but with the conditions under which certain highly general concepts – like the concept of other minds or of the existence of body in general – have application, given that such concepts play a key role in entire discourses and are central to our thought and talk as a whole. That is, the aim of a TA is to provide a 'deduction' (in Kant's sense) of such concepts by showing their indispensability to our having the experience we do, and to anything's having anything which we can recognise as experience. What a TA *shows* is how fundamental beliefs like the belief in the existence of body work in our conceptual scheme, by showing how talk of our experience carries essential reference to concepts deployed in having that experience, and without which that experience would not be possible (= would not make sense, would be unintelligible). What is typical of TAs proper is that they purport to establish the conditions necessary for experience, or experience of a certain kind, *as a whole*; and, at their most controversial, to establish a conclusion about the nature and existence of the external world, or other minds, as these – and particularly the world's existence – can be derived in consequence of paying attention to what *has* to be the case for there to be *experience*, or in order for experience to be as it is. This is the feature of Kant's transcendental efforts (and indeed the force of his calling them *transcendental* is explained by this feature) which, as noted above, roused interest or indignation among his successors; for the claim here is a substantial one indeed.

The problem in hand, then, is to give an account of TAs in this weightier and more challenging sense. The issues which need to be dealt with are various. One is whether there is a special, new, unique, or otherwise different kind of logic at work in a TA. Some writers suggest that this must be so, and in consequence raise questions about the validity of TAs or at very least about the status of their premisses. Other writers, again, deny the validity or alternatively the value of TAs on the grounds that they turn on covertly suppressed empirical premisses, or on a version of the verification principle, an objection made familiar by Stroud's work. Another issue concerns what kind of conclusion TAs, if valid, can be hoped to yield; for in the primary literature there is a sharp distinction between a more and a less ambitious construal of what in the end TAs might prove. The options range, briefly, from the hope that TAs might prove the existence of the external world, as just noted, to the hope that they might show that certain concepts are necessary to our conceptual scheme. Clearly these are two quite different results; and the latter option involves the further problem, whether our conceptual scheme is the only possible one, or just one among a number of alternatives. This problem, regarding uniqueness, has been raised by Mackie and Korner.

Although it would look to be more appropriate to deal with these two sets of questions about TAs in the order just sketched, it in fact works better to take them in reverse order. In other words, settling, what we might hope to achieve by means of TAs provides insight into questions about their structure, as will become apparent.

It is instructive to make a general survey of the two kinds of outcomes which TAs might yield, and to investigate what is involved in each. First, the difficulty to which TAs are addressed is most pointedly characterised as the standard sceptical challenge concerning what justification we have, if any, for employing the concepts of an external world which we do standardly employ. In Kant it is, for example, causal necessitation and the existence of objects, in Strawson it is, for example, particular identity, which provide the focus for the sceptical challenge and which their employment of a TA is designed to meet. Depending on how optimistic one is about TAs, the options are: (A) that one might prove the existence of the external world (i.e. of objects in some systematic relation) and thus settle the sceptic's doubts outright, or (B) that one might prove that the concept of objects is indispensable to our having experience, or to our having experience of a certain kind, and thus meet the sceptic's challenge at least as far as our conceptual scheme is concerned. To settle the sceptic's doubts outright under option B one would then and further have to show that our conceptual scheme is the only possible or conceivable one. Although option B states a weaker requirement on what a TA should yield than does A, it is more complex, but this does not mean it is more difficult; if anything, A appears on the face of it the more difficult of the two to achieve.

Regarding option A, matters are as follows. The chief difficulty A faces is satisfying the sceptic on this point: that even if it were shown that it is a necessary condition of our having coherent experience that we have and can employ concepts with objective reference, it still needs to be shown that the possession of such concepts entails that something 'out there' in an objective world answers to them – or, alternatively but equivalently put, that it is a necessary condition of our having such concepts that there be objects to which these concepts apply. It is one thing to show that, given some suitable characterisation of our experience which the sceptic will not find independently objectionable, we can derive the necessity of employing concepts of, say, some or all of objects, space, time, and causality, and quite another, or further, thing to show that there are items, events, and characteristics of them, answering to these concepts and yet existentially independent of their use.

A major part of the difficulty in this connection resides in the fact that, even in advance of offering an actual TA, it looks as if nothing like option A can be successfully worked out by reasoning from the fact that there is experience, or from some richer premiss characterising that experience, to talk about the way things are independently of that experience but which is a necessary condition of it, *without* either (1) supplementing the argument by additional factual premisses, or (2) (and a little less tendentiously) arguing that it is somehow just constitutive of the meaning or significance of the concept-introducing terms employed that they have empirical conditions of application under which, and only under which, they can be known to be truly applied. On the first point: the status of supplementary factual premisses will be highly suspect from the sceptic's point of view, and it is not at all clear that one escapes a taint of sophism if one admits them even in prospect. If such premisses assert nothing more than this or that is how our experience seems to us (that is, if they merely reiterate or extend the initial premiss), they do not take us beyond experience to objects. If they assert something about the world, or our experience's connection with the world, then either (and most likely) they will simply invite sceptical challenge of the sort the TA is itself trying to meet, or they will beg the question by being true in a *merely* internal sense – that is they will be true only if there is a world, or true only on condition that we assume such a world. Either way they do not further the objectives of option A.

As to the second point: to rely upon a verification principle would seem – if Stroud is right – to render otiose the apparatus of a TA itself, for if the weight of a TA is to be borne by a verification principle, one might as well dispense with the former and rely on the latter alone. Moreover, even if one were to weaken a verification principle so far that it was indistinguishable from some such general 'principle of significance' as Strawson finds in Kant, namely that 'there is no legitimate or even meaningful employment of ideas or concepts which does not relate them to empirical or experiential conditions of their application' (*Bounds of Sense*, p. 16), it would still be the case that merely specifying such conditions would not of itself tell us, or show us, that in the satisfaction of these conditions a concept in fact succeeded in applying to something objective. The reason is that such a verification principle could be satisfied by experience even in an ideal universe. Just so long as experience in such a universe is systematic, and there are criteria for distinguishing coherently in discourse between what is 'subjective' and 'objective' (for example my memories from tables), then we have the equipment of objectivity concepts, and the experiential conditions for their application, without a concommitant realist ontology; we can employ such concepts 'legitimately', that is, in such a way as for them to be basic both to the course of our experience and the body of judgments we make about it, without there being a world independent of our thought of it. (It is perhaps not fortuitous that some commentators on antirealism, which introduces a related principle of significance for terms in a language or part of a language, have elected to see idealism as the outcome of taking such a line. Putnam is one such commentator.[5])

The idea that a principle of empirical significance could be employed as a criterion for sense or conceptual intelligibility in an ideal universe is worth dwelling upon for a moment, for two reasons. One is that it explains the force of sceptical appeals to the evil demon in Descartes and the mad scientist in Unger, an analogue of which occurs in Walker's remarks on what use a verification principle might have or fail to have in securing against transcendental idealism.[6] The other is that it shows, at least partly, what sense attaches to the notion of a 'possible experience'. Briefly, the sense is that characterising a possible experience comes down to giving a consistent account or description of experience which 'saves the appearances', even perhaps to the extent of saving Aristotle's 'endoxa', the commonly-held assumptions and beliefs in a conceptual scheme at a time. A quick sketch of an ideal experience might go like this (and I repeat, in essentials, the sketch given in Chapter 2 above): concepts of what in realist terminology would be called 'subjective' and 'objective' elements in experience may be characterised as belonging to (say) two different conceptual categories in the idealist's scheme, such that concepts in the 'objective' category, call it the O-category, like concepts of tables and stones, differ from those in the 'subjective' category, call it the S-category, like one's own images, memories, and desires, in virtue of such features as that O-concepts are far less tractable to one's willings than S-concepts; that they are linked together in more determinate fashion than S-concepts, so that their relations may be represented as law-like;

[5] H. Putnam, 'Reference and understanding' in *Meaning and the Moral Sciences*, London 1978, pp. 97-117.

[6] Walker, *Kant*, pp. 124-5.

that thoughts intending O-type accusatives differ in *quality* from S-type ones, perhaps – in Humean fashion – by being more 'forceful' and 'vivid', say; and so on. Then for allocation to the relevant class of the kind of reference the idealist takes his concepts to have, it will be possible to state that some concept is of such-and-such a kind just according to whether it satisfies the criteria for a concept to be of that kind in general. Such criteria are readily and naturally to be based on what the course of that experience is itself like.

As one would expect, the bare bones of a characterisation like this carry barely any plausibility without a further gloss. Consider, parenthetically, what kind of gloss might be given to the least plausible point above, regarding what it would take to make intelligible the idea that the presumption of objectivity in our pre-theoretical conceptual scheme is adequately saved by the idea that O-concepts are concepts of *objects* because their accusatives are 'less tractable to our willings' than those of S-concepts. There is a neglected germ of an idea in Berkeley's first *Dialogue* on this score. Pre-theoretically, the fact that the world appears to be largely intractable to one's willings suggests that it is independent of one's will, and so of one's thought. But this is not an argument, or at any rate not a successful argument, for the world's independence of one's thought; it is a merely psychological consideration. The most it can do is to add to the plausibility of a 'simplest hypothesis' view like Mackie's as to the world's being the case. But this is not good enough, for the short reason that the simplicity of our hypotheses is logically compatible with their falsity. If the willing argument is to be a successful argument, it must admit of supplementary premisses enabling one to move from the fact that O-concepts are independent of one's will to their being independent of one's thought, which would have to account for such facts as that all one's willings are only some of one's thoughts, and – as a psychiatrist might point out – not all one's thoughts (and that includes S-type ones) are subject to one's willings anyway.

In any event, the point about such arguments as these for an idealist case is that they show that importing a verification principle into a TA will not be sufficient to deliver the goods which option A contracted to supply, namely, a demonstration of the fact that experience requires objects of a relevantly objective, that is non-ideal, kind. Since a TA *without* some version of a verification principle is even less likely to do so, option A invites pessimism.

What, then, of option B? To begin with, B looks relatively homely in comparison to A. There is no special difficulty attaching to the task of exhibiting and investigating the necessary preconditions of our experience, especially experience as it is *in fact* conceptualised by us. We are entitled at the very least to claim attention for investigations into the notions of objects, time, space, and causality, given that it at least seems to us that our experience is of a world of causally-interactive spatio-temporal continuants. If we have and can apply the concept of an object, then we have certain other concepts, for example that of the continued unperceived existence of objects, which is a necessary condition for our being able to reidentify objects and so of our concept of an object itself. This particular line of thought is familiar from Strawson and Stroud's criticism of Strawson. Now, showing that we must have a certain concept does not entail that anything in a putative 'out there' answers to it; possession does not guarantee 'objective reference' in Strawson's sense, although it does in Kant's 'transcendentally ideal' sense. The point of Stroud's criticism was just that Strawson's attempt upon securing 'objective reference' of a realist sort needed a verification principle; and for the reasons given in connection with option A, this will not in any case work. In fact, the difference between options A and B is just the difference between giving an account of the necessary conditions of our experience in terms of what is the case in the world (option A) or in terms of what concepts we must have and apply if that experience is to be possible (option B). Whereas in A a route has to be engineered *from* the concepts whose possession constitutes the necessary conditions for our experience *to* the world, in B no such route is sought.

But option B, of course, would indeed be a homely affair if all that we needed to do was to lay out and inspect the necessary preconditions of our having the experience we in fact at present enjoy. Just doing this and no more would have a certain parochial interest, to be sure; but it tells us very little about experience *in general*, and nothing about ontology, so that its philosophical interest would be limited, and as a way of meeting scepticism it would be irrelevant. Relevance enters only when it is claimed of some account given under option B that the necessary conditions revealed are necessary to *all* experience; and this claim is equivalent to a claim about the uniqueness of our conceptual scheme, at least in its basics.

It is against this claim that Mackie and Korner direct their chief criticisms of TAs.[7] What their criticisms come down to is that it is impossible to specify in advance of knowing anything about what an alternative conceptual scheme might be like, that any alternative conceptual scheme would be impossible. This says that no sense attaches to the locutions 'only possible' or 'only conceivable' conceptual scheme in general, still less, of course, as applied to our own scheme from within.

There are two counters to this criticism. The first derives directly from the arguments against relativism stated in Chapter 3 above. To recapitulate briefly: one recognises that a conceptual scheme is a language or set of intertranslatable languages, so that criteria of identity for conceptual schemes just consist in the translation relations obtaining between the languages in the set. Along lines developed from Davidson's views and discussed at length above, one then tackles, *not* the question of the uniqueness of a scheme but, instead, the issue of a criterion of languagehood. It turns out on this tack that the criterion of languagehood is: translatability into a familiar idiom. The reason, in summary form, is that if anything is to count as a language for us, it must have certain recognisable and renderable devices for assent, dissent, individuation, and attribution, and a concomittant presupposed plural ontology of individuals as the referents of the individuating devices, which in turn are the satisfiers of the attributive devices. If strings of sounds or marks contained nothing whatever that could be recognised as having or allowing these roles, it could not count as a language for us. It follows from taking account of the nature of languagehood, and translatability as the criterion of languagehood, that in so far as 'conceivable conceptual scheme' or 'conceivable experience' means 'a conceptual scheme or experience admitting of an intelligible and consistent description', anything that will so count will be so describable in terms of the concepts we in fact employ. To put the matter another way: to understand an alternative scheme *as* an alternative scheme, there must be sufficiently rich mappings from our own to the alien scheme to allow us to see that there are differences and *ipso facto* what they are; but this presupposes there being enough

[7] Korner, op. cit., passim; Mackie, *Cement of the Universe*, pp. 96ff.

in common between the two schemes to allow comparisons. Thus the very idea of an alternative scheme depends on a shared range of concepts, and these, as the languagehood considerations just adduced show, will be central and basic concepts at that. It follows that 'alternative' in 'alternative scheme' can only refer to superstructural rather than basic features, and accordingly that all experience recognisable as such by us has certain basic and pervasive features on which our recognition of that experience *as* experience turns.

As put by Mackie, the objection to a uniqueness claim takes the form of saying that it is a result of merely contingent limitations upon our imaginative abilities that we discount the idea of alternative schemes if they do not share at least some of our own scheme's core concepts. Thus there might be experience of a kind so radically different from our own that we cannot recognise it as such; but it will still be experience for all that. The second counter-argument deals with this form of the objection. One quick way to deal with the objection is to restate the argument just given, of course, for an alternative formulation of it apt for this case is to say that any conceptual scheme, or form of experience, which was totally sealed off from our ability even to recognise it as such, cannot make a jot of difference to us; such possibilities are, as it were, empty. This is true, but a trifle cavalier, for it does not address itself to the precise point about the contingent limits of our imaginative powers. More respectfully, then, one needs to show what force 'conceivable' is to have in 'conceivable experience', in particular by distinguishing 'conceivable' from 'imaginable'. Descartes provides a useful hint by means of his chiliagon example: we might be able to conceive of a thousand-sided figure and a nine-hundred-and-ninety-eight-sided figure as having certain determinate characteristics and, in consequence of these, certain determinate differences with respect to each other; but, quite evidently, one could not *imagine* two figures – these two – in such a way as to allow one qualitatively to distinguish between them in one's imagination. The reason for the difference is that *conceiving* something comes down to being able to articulate and defend an account or description of that thing, in particular in a way which is consistent with our conceptions of related items, whereas imagining something, or that something is the case, need not involve us in giving (and having to give) an account parasitic upon the concepts by means of which the required account is to be set up if it is to be set up consistently. For example, I can imagine myself a wealthy and handsome fellow, but conceiving the coming-to-be of a situation in which I am in fact such a fellow would involve essential appeal to some process of change consistent with the way things are with me now – as, let us say, the arrival of a telegram from Vernon's Football Pools, followed by a visit to the plastic surgeon, and so on. *Mutatis mutandis*, this applies exactly to conceiving conceptualised experiencings.

If the foregoing sketches of counterarguments to the uniqueness criticism work, and B-option TAs tell us what are the necessary conceptual presuppositions of what recognisably counts as experience, then the terminus we arrive at under option B is a rather interesting one. At its best such a result would consist in a claim to the effect that experience necessarily presupposes the possession and deployment of this or these concepts. The focal example is that of a concept of objects; so, to say that we must have and deploy a concept of objects is to say that we must think there are objects, or assume there are objects, in order for coherent or intelligible experience to be possible. In view of the fact that under option B this entails nothing further, in particular nothing further about objects existing in total independence of our experience of them, most commentators would conclude that B-option TAs are of little value. This would reflect the hearty realist impulses which govern our ambitions for philosophy. It seems to me on the contrary that something most interesting results.

The sceptic's challenge concerns what justification we have for our beliefs about the world, especially those beliefs which commit us to a pre-theoretical ontology of things enduring through time independently of our perceiving them. Under option A we would, if successful, have justified these beliefs directly. Under option B we provide a justification with an important difference of texture; which difference captures precisely, I think, what Kant intended by his legal metaphor, and what Hume and Wittgenstein meant by charging scepticism with idleness. If the beliefs in question are necessarily presupposed to our conceptual scheme, and if our conceptual scheme is the only conceivable one, then the beliefs in question are more than justified; we are shown to be unable to do without them. And that is enough to defeat scepticism. Naturally, the sceptic will be tempted to complain that the question at issue is not whether we have to assume such beliefs, but whether they are *true*, in the sense that these beliefs are about objects which are '*really* real', *totally* independent of our experience. Here is the interesting result of the B-option TA: it shows this kind of question to be misguided. There *is* nothing more to be said about the status of objects than follows from the fact that we have to assume the applicability of our concepts of objects. This is interesting because it forces a limit to the amount of ontological weight than can be borne by the items in the domain over which our thought and talk range, with a concomittant change in what kind of philosophical gloss upon our pre-theoretical ontology we are to feel able to give. In schematic terms, ontological weight increases with existential independence; to say that objects are no more than what we must have concepts of for coherent experience, is to acknowledge that objects are not as ontologically heavy as we thought; we find ourselves having to espouse the slim maiden of an idealism rather than the plump dame of realism. This is the key to understanding the notion of empirical realism in Kant, which is the theory of the world our conceptual apparatus commits us to when viewed from the standpoint of transcendental idealism, which constitutes the metatheory in terms of which this commitment is described. (I will not now go into this point, because it is a large issue, but it provokes this thought: that if, on analogy with the results here, one were to give an account of contemporary antirealism as an 'empirical realism' in roughly the Kantian sense, then contemporary realism would turn out to occupy the 'transcendental realist' slot in the Kantian sense. The '*really* real' issue, that question shown to be misguided by the result of a B-option TA, is just the question which a transcendental realist is eager to put and have answered; there are links here with the contemporary realist idea that there must be determinate states of affairs existing independently of our cognising them for it to be the case that some area of discourse is meaningful, since the meaning of a sentence is to be given by stating its verification-transcendent truth-conditions.)

In short, then, sceptical doubt is shown to be idle or pointless because the beliefs the sceptic asks us to justify turn out to be necessary to our thought and talk of the world, and nothing counts as thought and talk unless it is recognisable as such from the standpoint of the thought and talk we enjoy; so that the beliefs to which we are committed, and to which essential reference must be made for any explanation or description of experience in general, are simply not negotiable, that is, are not open to doubt. One might extend the legal metaphor suggested by Kant's 'deduction' and say that the terminus of the argument here is the *defeasance* of scepticism; one renders sceptical doubt null and void by a demonstration of the fact that we are bound to hold the beliefs the sceptic asks us to justify.

The other problem that needs to be dealt with in saying what TAs are and what they can do is the question whether they turn upon a special or new kind of logic, or whether there is anything peculiar about their form. In a way this is a rather puzzling question to ask at all, for in regard to all other modes of reasoning – deduction, induction, the uses of analogy and example, even the assembling of reminders – it is not on the whole a question (except for philosophers of logic as such) whether some general form of reasoning will do, but rather whether a given particular argument will do. Some analogical reasonings will be persuasive, and some not; some deductions will be sound, others unsound. Each argument stands or falls by its own merits. No more is required of a TA than that it should assert that there is experience, or experience of a certain character, and then state under what conditions experience, or such experience, is possible. The conditions under which something is possible are its necessary conditions; and accordingly a TA is a process of displaying the necessary conditions of something's being the case. Evidentally the initial premiss will be synthetic and the later premisses and conclusion analytic with respect to it, but that creates no problem, and certainly does not involve a special or innovative logic. From the formal point of view, the logic of necessary conditionality is given or displayed by modus ponens, modus tollens, and the rule of implication; indeed, the list is redundant, for any one will do to show or display the relation, formally considered, in which a necessary condition stands to what it conditions. But formal considerations do not exhaust the sense in which, to display the necessary conditions for something x's being the case, is what it is to 'unpack' x, as we are fond of saying; and this is not merely a matter of finding a way of explaining x or giving the sense of the expressions by which the concept x is introduced, but – more – of showing in what possession and application of *x* consists.

In a sense, the expression transcendental *argument* is therefore misleading, for it suggests one particular kind of licensed movement from premisses to conclusion, representable as an inference with a single identifiable form. It is, rather, more informative to talk instead of TAs in this way: to argue, or reason, or proceed transcendentally, or to employ standard philosophical techniques transcendentally, is just to argue or proceed, etc., with a certain aim in mind and a certain subject-matter to hand. This indeed is Strawson's view; that there is nothing distinctive about the form of TAs, and that what *is* distinctive about them is their aim and subject-matter. The subject-matter is experience; the aim is to trace links and dependences among the experiential concepts we employ, with a view to seeing which are basic and how they are so.[8]

On this view, it is quite misguided to expend energy along Wilkerson's lines by trying to argue that a TA is an argument which, although deductively invalid as he discovers his own particular example of one to be, might none the less be thought to state the conditions sufficient *ceteris paribus* and such that we cannot imagine any others, for something's being the case.[9] Taking this kind of view results from certain worries that Wilkerson, in common with some others, feels about the idea that TAs are, as it were, merely unravellings of what must be the case given a successful conceptual practice – focally, the making of empirical judgments. This is that if TAs proceed by analytic steps to the necessary conditions of that practice, they must somehow be at best trivial and anyway circular, in the sense that everything the TA tells us must already be tucked away in the concept of that practice. But this is to mistake both the value of any enterprise which tells us what is implicated in the use of some concepts, and the complexity (and at the same time importance) of some of the concepts typically at issue in TA investigations. Even if, as is of course the case, whatever comes out of an unravelling of a concept was already in a sense there to begin with, the process of making quite clear what was already there can be highly informative and consequential.

A further worry is one already met with, that if TAs are *analytic* investigations of the necessary conditions of the applicability of a

[8] Strawson, lectures and conversations, Oxford 1976-81.
[9] Wilkerson, *Kant's Critique of Pure Reason*, ch. 10 passim; cf. pp. 200-2.

concept, then the terminus of the investigations will turn out to relate only to the relative necessity of holding some further concept to be applicable, with no substantial results to show about the way things are either absolutely or 'out there' (for the realist these will be the same). As I have already hinted, there are no good reasons to be disappointed on this score, for such a result offers excitement in a different direction.

One final worry which may lie in the background of reservations about TAs is that what they purport to reveal in the way of what is *basic* to experience is itself highly complex and richly textured, namely beliefs about persisting perception-independent particulars – about which there can be considerable debate, for example as to whether they are events or otherwise; as to their identity-criteria; as to whether these latter carry reference to essences; and so on. But these issues are not a concern here. It is not a requirement on something's being *basic* that it also be *simple*; nor is it a condition upon identifying a certain range of beliefs as basic that one must exhaustively settle the question of what it is their complexity consists in. That (that is, their *analysis*) is a further matter; what is alone at issue here is the question of what *role* such beliefs play in our conceptual scheme. The most that one would expect from an investigation into what role such beliefs play is that it will suggest what directions such an analysis might take.

I conclude then by remarking that the portrayal of TAs given here is of a fairly low-key kind. TAs are nothing special in virtue of their form, being distinctive only in virtue of their content and aims. The B-option TAs are those which, in conjunction with antirelativist arguments, do the required work; they do not prove the existence of objects independently of experience, but reveal what the basic structure of our conceptual scheme is like, in the particular sense that they show what concepts are indispensably presupposed to experience – that is, which are required for experience which is intelligible to, or describable by, or recognisable *as* experience by us. And I hinted that this has consequences for other and allied concerns in philosophy which, at present anyway, are somewhat unfashionable. (Namely, that some form of antirealism of an idealist stamp looks to be the natural outcome of this line of thought; saying which connects with the comment at the end of the preceding paragraph regarding what direction an analysis of our beliefs might take.)

It is now appropriate to look in detail at the distinction between options A and B and how the B-option TA does the work required of it, by applying the distinction in an analysis of particular TAs. The TAs I select as case-studies are suggested by Strawson in *Individuals*; one concerns other minds, the other concerns the unperceived continued existence of particulars. This latter argument is central to my concerns here, but I (very briefly) canvass the former as well because it shows up certain features of B-option TAs which it is important to note.

Strawson argued that one can ascribe states of consciousness to oneself only if one is able to ascribe them to others, and that the fact that this is so defeats scepticism about other minds.[10] For, to doubt the existence of other minds the sceptic must employ the concept of other minds itself, which can only be done if he distinguishes between 'my states of consciousness' and 'others' states of consciousness'; and this can only be done, in turn, if others exist, because the identification of conscious states can only be affected by reference to particulars of a special kind, viz. persons, the concept of which – in turn again – demands that there be criteria for distinguishing one person from another, for otherwise the identification of states of consciousness would not be possible. So one can talk of '*my* experiences' only if one can talk of others' experiences; this is possible only if there are criteria for distinguishing between persons; and since one *does* talk significantly about one's own experience, there must be such criteria. Then if there are such criteria, bodily behaviour constitutes logically adequate grounds for ascription of states of consciousness to others. Hence the sceptic's doubts are idle, Strawson concludes, because he cannot so much as formulate those doubts without employing the discourse whose very conditions of employment legitimise what he wishes to call into question.

The other-minds sceptic need not appear to be wholly without recourse in the face of this argument, however, for it seems open to him to say that whereas one must indeed have the concept of others' experience in order to have a concept of 'my own' experience, and whereas experiences are indeed identified only by reference to bodies, nevertheless the most that this entails is that one has to *conceive*

[10] Strawson, *Individuals*, ch. 3 passim; cf. p. 106.

of the possibility of others' experience, and that *if* there are any others' experiences then we can identify them only by reference to bearers of M- and P-predicates: but it does not establish *that there are* any experiencing others. In other words, the sceptic's charge can be seen to be that Strawson fails to distinguish the conditions under which a concept is intelligible (under which a term has meaning) from the conditions of its successful empirical application;[11] it can be allowed that one must know what it would be like to other-ascribe states of consciousness, but to concede that one must possess certain concepts is not to concede that one has criteria enabling one to employ the relevant concept-introducing terms in true statements.[12]

This counter-argument by the sceptic is highly interesting, not least because it again reveals the respect in which a tendency to realism in the theory of meaning is misguided. For the sceptic is saying that it is one thing to understand the meaning of a term, and another thing to apply, or to be able to apply, that term, or to know when a successful application of the term has been effected. But this is to force a gap between understanding and use which simply will not do. It is a very minimal condition on what it is for someone S to grasp the meaning of a term W that S is able to use or employ W, which can be put either by saying (the following two formulations are equivalent) that S's being able to use W depends upon his knowing the assertibility-conditions for W, or that S knows the rules governing W's use. The rules governing the use of empirical terms include those which correlate the term to empirical situations – that is, situations in S's experience – recognisable by S, in which the term, if it is significant, is applicable; so any situation in which S in fact makes *proper* use of W will be one in which S knows both (a) that W is applicable in such situations and (b) that this is such a situation; this is precisely what confers warrant on S's use of W in that situation (see Chapter 2 above). Therefore to 'understand the meaning' of a term *just is* (*at least*) to be able to apply it; and the term in question is significant only if there are situations in which it can be applied.[13] Accordingly the other-minds sceptic fails in his

[11] Cf. K. Ward, 'The ascription of experiences', *Mind* 79 (1970), pp. 415-20; and A.J. Ayer, *The Concept of a Person*, London 1963, passim.

[12] Cf. G.W. Smith, 'The concepts of the sceptic', *Philosophy* 49 (1974) pp. 153-4.

[13] This again recalls Kant's 'principle of significance'.

counter-argument to Strawson's thesis, for if possession of a concept (understanding the meaning of a term) just is at least to know how to apply it, and if the concept has content only if there are situations in which it can be applied, then there is no gap of the kind the sceptic is trying to force.

However, the sceptic will take it that the reply just given to his counter-argument constitutes a strong verificationist thesis, for he takes it that the point of the TA is to *prove* that there are other minds independently of our possession of the concept of other minds; which is to say, he takes it that the TA is an option-A TA. Nevertheless it is evident that the 'principle of significance' upon which the argument partly turns is very much weaker than the verification principle the sceptic has in mind, and accordingly does not and cannot amount to a claim about existence in the 'really real' sense; nothing follows *or is claimed to follow* about the existence of other minds in the absolute sense demanded by the sceptic, that is, the existence of other minds independently of our having grounds to assert anything about other minds. What *is* claimed is that we cannot make sense of the idea of the family of concepts including 'persons' and 'my own states of consciousness' without essentially employing the concept of other minds; that we do indeed make sense of such concepts; and that, accordingly, it is wholly fruitless and idle to raise such sceptical doubts on the point in question.[14] This result differs from bare content with the concessions made by the sceptic to Strawson's original argument (viz. that having the concept of other minds is essential to ascribing consciousness to oneself), by showing that what the sceptic *then* goes on to require via the 'understanding'-'applying' dichotomy (namely that proof be furnished, in the absolute sense, of other minds) is illegitimate, because there is no such dichotomy, and hence there is no more to be said; further demands are pointless.

Applying this strategy to Stroud's reformulation of Strawson's argument about the unperceived continued existence of particulars illuminates the issues there too. Strawson[15] characterises the sceptic's position on this score as being that he illegitimately

[14] It is doubtful whether Strawson originally saw the argument in this light; my understanding is that he does so now. Lectures and conversations, Oxford 1976-81.

[15] Cf. *Individuals*, pp. 34-6; also 77-8, 109.

'pretends to accept a conceptual scheme, but at the same time quietly rejects one of the conditions of its employment ... his doubts are unreal ... because they amount to the rejection of the whole conceptual scheme within which alone such doubts make sense' (*Individuals*, p. 35). The sceptic is therefore either in a self-contradictory situation, or he may be 'muddledly' advocating a different scheme (p. 36; cf. p. 78). The reason is that 'we have the idea of a single spatio-temporal system of material things' in which objects are variously related, and that 'a *condition* of our having this conceptual scheme is the unquestioning acceptance of particular-identity in at least some cases of non-continuous observation' (ibid.). For if we supposed that we never reidentified particulars, then we should have the idea of discrete, independent spatio-temporal systems for each new stretch of observation. But if so there could be no question of doubt about the identity of an item in one system with an item in another. Doubt of a sceptical kind 'makes sense only if the two systems are not independent'; but then it is 'precisely the condition (of a unified system) that there should be satisfiable and commonly satisfied criteria for the identity of at least some items in one subsystem with some items in the other', and hence the sceptic is in an untenable situation; for to raise his doubts at all he must accept our conceptual scheme but deny one of its conditions (p. 36). The argument has it that, effectively, the proposition 'objects continue to exist unperceived' is entailed by or is otherwise specially related to our conceptual scheme. The crucial question concerns what is to be understood by saying that this proposition is thus entailed or otherwise related; my contention is that to say this is not to claim that objects are '*really* real' in the absolute sense demanded by the sceptic, for such a claim makes no sense; rather, it is to say that the proposition has something like Wittgenstein's 'grammatical' status, and thus perhaps that it is better described as 'presupposed' by our conceptual scheme, in a sense I shall later make clear.

First, however, it is necessary to examine Stroud's criticism of Strawson's argument, which Stroud regards as furnishing a test-case for (at any rate contemporary) TAs in general (op. cit. p. 120). Stroud takes Strawson's argument to start from the premiss

(1) We think of the world as containing objective particulars in a single spatio-temporal system;

from which is to be derived the proposition doubted or denied by the sceptic, viz.

(6) Objects continue to exist unperceived (p. 245).

Strawson's strategy is to show that 6 is a necessary condition of 1, which latter is a description or characterisation of our conceptual scheme. From 1 can be derived immediately two further premisses:

(2) If we think of the world as containing objective particulars in a single spatio-temporal system, then we are able to identify and reidentify particulars.

(3) If we can reidentify particulars, then we must have satisfiable criteria on the basis of which to make reidentifications (p. 246).

This is the point at which Strawson himself stops, Stroud says, and evidently 1-3 do not jointly yield 6; so there must be further, suppressed, steps in the argument. Premisses 1-3 at most show that 'if the sceptic's statements make sense then we must have satisfiable criteria on the basis of which we can reidentify a presently observed object as numerically the same as one observed earlier' (ibid.); but this is not enough, for the sceptic can still claim that it is possible that all our reidentifications are mistaken. A principle that would rule out this possibility would be:

(4) If we know that the best criteria for reidentification have been satisfied, then we know that objects continue to exist unperceived (ibid.).

But the conjunction of 1-4 is a verification principle; 'if the notion of objective particulars makes sense to us then we can sometimes know certain conditions to be fulfilled, the fulfilment of which logically implies either that objects continue to exist unperceived or they do not' (p. 247). This principle is necessary for the derivation of 6, but not sufficient; nevertheless, in Stroud's view, the verification principle is of itself, if it is independently satisfactory, sufficient to refute the sceptic, for 'if the sceptic's claim makes sense it must be false, since if the proposition could not be known to be true or false it would make no sense' (ibid.). However, to fulfil the original plan of deriving 6, one further premiss is needed:

(5) We sometimes know that the best criteria we have for the reidentification of particulars have been satisfied (ibid.).

Unhappily, although 6 now follows from 1-5, Strawson's project of defeating the sceptic by demonstrating that his doubts fail to make sense, cannot be accomplished, for 5 is a factual premiss which is not about our conceptual scheme. Had 6 followed from premisses only about our conceptual scheme, then the sceptic would have been shown to be doubting necessary conditions of its coherence or intelligibility. But since the doubt or denial of 6 does not involve the rejection of our conceptual scheme alone, says Stroud, the sceptic may be making sense after all.

In Stroud's view, the move to 5 is not only self-defeating but unnecessary owing to 4. Premiss 5 was to constitute the final step in a TA; but with the addition of 4 to 1-3 the sceptic is directly refuted by a verification principle, if such a principle is valid, and this means that, first, step 5 is otiose, and secondly, that the argument as a whole turns upon its embedded verification principle, without which it would have no appearance of bite at all. Accordingly 'there is no need to go through an indirect or transcendental argument' at all (p. 242).

What Stroud takes to follow from this analysis of Strawson's argument he expresses best in a later source ('Transcendental arguments and "epistemological naturalism" ' pp. 112-14). Kant's efforts in the first *Critique* would, if successful, have shown that certain truths or principles have a special status, as making experience or thought possible. Denying these principles would indeed violate the necessary conditions of the denial's itself making sense. The problem is to show 'whether any such rich and interesting "principles" can ever be shown to have (the) exalted status' which Kant claimed for them (p. 113). The difficulty with Kant's own efforts in this direction arises in large part from his transcendental psychology, regarded as objectionable by almost all subsequent commentators; but, in Stroud's view, modern efforts (like Strawson's) to arrive at Kant's results have not had much to offer in place of his transcendental psychology (p. 114). Indeed they founder because they substitute 'an ungrounded appeal to a general principle of meaning or significance, according to which concepts are intelligible to us only if we know the empirical conditions under which they could be truly and knowingly applied' (ibid.) – that is, a verification principle; and Stroud says of such a principle that it 'seems to me implausible in fact as an account of the intelligibility or significance of particular propositions, and, more importantly, it would deny or render superfluous the very special project Kant set himself'. It would do this latter because if we were armed with such a principle we would find no sceptical doubt threatening; the principle would 'endow *every* intelligible proposition with ... privileged epistemic status, and so there would be no need to discover a special central core or a fundamental set of "principles" which are necessary for all thought and experience' (ibid.).

Finally, Stroud remarks that if TAs of the kind Strawson devised are offered without any use being made of a verification principle, then the most that could be proved by a consideration of the necessary conditions for experience and talk is 'that, for example, we must *believe* that there are material objects and other minds if we are to be able to speak meaningfully at all'; that is, it will not have been shown that *there are* material objects (p. 257). In summary, then, Stroud holds that TAs turn on a verification principle which, if valid, renders TAs themselves unnecessary; that the verification principle is implausible; and that TAs without an embedded verification principle can at most show what we have to believe, not how things are, regarding the objects of perceptual experience or other minds.

Examining Stroud's arguments provides us with exactly what we require to complete this essay's project against scepticism. What has happened here is that Stroud has taken Strawson's argument to be an option-A TA designed to prove the existence of objects in the realist sense; and in terms of his reconstruction of the argument with that objective in mind, the argument does indeed turn on a strong verification principle, it does indeed require the additional factual premiss 5, and accordingly it does indeed fail in the ways Stroud specifies. But Stroud's perception of Strawson's intentions is mistaken. He takes it that Strawson wished to prove the existence of the external world, and in general that any TA is of little value if it fails to do so. His views in this respect are illustrated by his saying: 'For Kant a TA is supposed to answer the question of "justification", and in so doing it demonstrates the "objective validity" of certain concepts. I have taken this to mean that the concept "X" has objective validity only if there are Xs and that demonstrating the objective validity of the concept is tantamount to demonstrating that Xs actually exist' (p. 256). As noted, Stroud then goes on to say that 'recent attempts to argue in analogous fashion' either depend on a verification principle, which is objectionable, or at most show that 'we must *believe* there are material objects' (ibid.), which, he holds, does not remove the problem of scepticism. On all these counts Stroud is mistaken.

To begin with, Strawson's intention is clearly revealed *not* to be what Stroud takes it to be, by his signposting his argument as follows: '... we have the idea of a single spatio-temporal system of material things ... Now I say that a *condition* of our having this conceptual scheme is the unquestioning acceptance of particular-identity in at least some cases of non-continuous observation' (*Individuals*, p. 36). This is not a claim about the existence of the external world; it is a claim to the effect that it is a necessary condition of thinking as we do that we *believe*, 'unquestioningly accept', that objects continue to exist unperceived. His argument is accordingly an option-B TA, and should be reconstructed accordingly. I turn to that shortly.

Secondly, Stroud's reading of Kant is starkly mistaken. One can only interpret Kant's talk of 'objective validity' in standard realist terms, as Stroud does, if one wholly ignores Kant's transcendental idealism, in the presence of which the Kantian concepts of 'justification' (= the right we have to employ certain concepts) and 'objective validity' are quite different from what Stroud makes of them. Talk of 'objects' in Kant is talk only of phenomenal objects (cf. A 104), and the 'objective validity' of an empirical concept is what it possesses if its employment is reflected in the rule-governed connectedness of representations (*Bounds of Sense*, p. 91). Given this, recent TAs like Strawson's are by no means so far unKantian as Stroud thought.

Thirdly, because option-B TAs are agnate to Kant's enterprise, no reliance is placed upon a verification principle in them, and indeed Stroud – although correct in his general intuition to the effect that an antirealist view of sense creeps in *somewhere* along the line – is mistaken both about the nature and the place of the constraint that empirical conditions play in talk of the sense of perceptual discourse. This point re-emerges below.

Finally, Stroud is mistaken about the power of option-B TAs against the sceptic. This point was made in the preceding discussion, but will be justified again below.

All Stroud's points, premissed as they are on the insistence that to defeat scepticism we must prove the truth of a realist view of the world, and so, collaterally, can rely only upon an option-A TA, reinforce one's inclination once again to take the view that it is epistemological, and its correlative linguistic, realism which is at fault in this domain of philosophy and which indeed generates the scepticism it is *ipso facto* unable to meet. Matters should rather be approached as follows.

The thrust of Strawson's argument can be stated best by looking at a criticism one might advance against an uncritical option-B reading of Stroud's reformulation of it. This is that on such a reading the argument looks to be in danger of collapse into triviality. Stroud identifies the first premiss as 'we think of the world as containing objective particulars in a single spatio-temporal system' and the option-B conclusion as 'we must think that objects continue to exist unperceived'. In line with Strawson's own (intentional) vagueness about the term 'particulars' (*Individuals*, p. 15) and the fact that Strawson uses that term interchangeably with 'material things' and 'item' in the presentation of his argument (p. 35), Stroud is under no obligation to be clear about what is to be understood by 'particulars' and 'objects' in his reformulation. Evidently however it is of some moment that these terms should be clear, for if 'particular' and 'material thing' are (for the purposes of the argument) equivalent, and if 'material thing' means 'material body' as it must, given that the operative term in both expressions is 'material', then Strawson's argument, on this reading of it, is such that its conclusion may not only be analytically but indeed *trivially* true, no additional premisses whatever being required to see how. For Strawson portrays our ordinary conception of 'material bodies' as spatial (indeed, tactual) entities satisfying requirements of 'richness, endurance, and stability' – the two latter properties both being temporal ones (pp. 34-40). Paraphrased in these terms, the first premiss, which is about how we ordinarily think, becomes 'we think of the world as containing objective, temporally enduring, and spatially extended particulars, in a single spatio-temporal system'. (Such a premiss would not be pleonastic since there could be spatio-temporal particulars in different, e.g. successive, spatio-temporal systems.) The 'temporally enduring' in the premiss is not problematic, for by itself it does not mean that objective material things continue to exist unperceived, merely that they endure. But what of 'objective'? There is no reasonable sense to be attached to 'objective' in this context other than 'independent of perception', for, banally, it is standardly contrasted to 'subjective' (what depends only on the subject's perceivings; what arises from or is found only in the subject's perceptual experience). But then the first premiss states: 'we think of the world as containing perception-independent, temporally enduring, spatially extended particulars in a single spatio-temporal system.' Trouble arises if, as it must, 'objects' in the conclusion means 'perception-independent, temporally enduring, spatially extended particulars'; for now the conclusion merely repeats part of the first premiss: it says 'we must think that perception-independent, temporally enduring, spatially extended particulars are perception-independent', and so is circularly – trivially – true. And yet the conclusion is meant to state a necessary condition of the first premiss. If this is the outcome of an option-B argument, it would be a vacuous option.

However, this is not what Strawson's argument comes down to. If the argument is to be one in which steps 1 and 6 are to say sufficiently different things for the derivation of 6 from 1 to be informative about the conditions necessary for the way we think about the world, the emphasis of the argument must be differently read. That is, either 6 must be saying something about what is a necessary condition for the *singleness* of the spatio-temporal system, or 1 must be saying something about the spatio-temporal *system*, i.e. its coherence and order, in the sense of the coherence of our experience; or both. I think it is clear that Strawson intended the main point to be the former of these options, for unless we can indeed reidentify particulars we should have no grounds for thinking of the world as a *single* spatio-temporal system; but this in turn connects with the question of the *coherence* of that system, and so one can fruitfully take it that Strawson's aim was to show that it is a condition of the *coherence* of the way we think that what we think of the world as being, viz. a spatio-temporal system, should be a *single* system; and that this in turn demands the unperceived continued existence of objects, in order that reidentifications of them can take place. The sceptic assumes the singleness of the system in order to talk of the way we think, but then doubts or denies the singleness of the system in doubting or denying a necessary condition of that way of thinking, namely that objects continue to exist when unperceived.

The point about reidentification is important, and it is here that Stroud locates the verification principle which would be required if the argument were an option-A TA. However the argument is an option-B TA, and runs as follows. If we think of the world as a single spatio-temporal system, and if this demands that we be able to reidentify particulars, then we must have (that is, it is a necessary condition of this way of thinking that we have) criteria for reidentifying particulars. If we think we have such criteria, then we must think (that is, it is a necessary condition of thinking that we possess such criteria) that they are satisfiable. If we think this, in turn, then we must think (i.e. it is a necessary condition of so thinking) that the items we reidentify by means of such criteria continue to exist when unperceived. There is no verification principle here; the terminus of the argument is that we must think, believe, or 'unquestioningly accept' that objects continue to exist unperceived. The premiss from which this statement of what we must think has been derived is, in effect, 'we coherently think of the world as a *single* spatio-temporal system of particulars', and states a necessary condition of our thinking in this way.

Stroud, as noted, concedes that a 'we must believe' result is obtainable, but does not think it is effective against scepticism. His reason is that the sceptic can with equanimity accept the necessity of believing this and that, and still deny that doing so delivers the (realist) epistemological goods. Neither would Mackie or Korner concede that this result defeats scepticism, as also noted, for the reason that what appears to have been derived is a *merely* conditional necessity, in the sense that it conditions only the way we happen to think of the world, or only experience as we in fact (at present, in this cultural context or in this phase of our conceptual history) happen to enjoy it; and that there could be and perhaps even are ways of thinking or experiencing which are not at all like ours. It is at this point that the antirelativist argument of Chapter 3 enters the picture, to demonstrate that a necessary condition for coherent experience is a necessary condition for experience *tout court*, for the conclusion of that argument is that nothing can count as experience which is not recognisable as such by us; which is to say, which does not have the same basic features as our own, for it is upon a community of shared features at this level that recognising anything as experience (a conceptual scheme or language) turns. This rebuttal of relativism also rebuts Stroud's realist-inclined sceptic; for if anything which counts for us as experience has as a necessary condition the belief in question, to doubt or deny that belief is *wholly* idle, since it infects the very idea of experience itself.

The reconstruction and amplification of Strawson's argument offered here in opposition to Stroud's reconstruction, together with the antirelativist argument of Chapter 3, thus constitute a satisfactory rebuttal of scepticism, a rebuttal just of the sort which this essay set out to provide; namely, a demonstration that the sceptical challenge is idle because, in the end, we cannot do otherwise than be committed to the belief which the sceptic challenges us to justify. It is not merely that we are entitled to this belief, but, more, we are absolutely bound to believe. However, there is a drawback to the argument as here presented. The drawback consists in the fact that the argument as it stands, owing to its generality, does not display in sufficient detail how belief in the continued unperceived existence of objects conditions experience; nor does it provide materials for how we are to think of objects and the nature of the experience which ranges over them. In particular, one wants to see what the sense of calling such a belief *basic* consists in. The argument in Chapter 2 was designed as a fuller version of this TA, with more background material relevant to a spelling out of these features. As there expressed, the argument is diffuse and enthymematic; so it is now appropriate to set it out schematically. Owing to the reconstruction and amplification of Strawson's argument just given, it is possible to do this in fairly brief compass.

The argument of Chapter 2 was aimed at showing that talk of the coherence of empirical experience is equivalent to talk of the sense of perceptual discourse, and that a necessary condition of our both having and being able to report empirical experience is that we believe there are objects in the full sense defined in Chapter 2, namely that they are perception-independent persisting spatial items.

Three connected conditions were specified as minimally necessary for the sense of perceptual discourse: that perceptual terms (that is terms, occurring in perceptual statements, which introduce concepts of objects and their properties) be correlated by a rule to items encountered in experience; that asserters of perceptual statements be able to recognise that given situations in their experience are ones in which given perceptual terms are so correlated; and that perceptual error be detectable and correctable in at least most cases. It was then argued that the crucial element here is the notion of the asserter's recognising items and features in his experience, and recognising them (if this is different) as those to which certain perceptual terms apply. What is required here is not an account of how as a matter of psychological and/or historical fact anyone comes to make the perceptual discriminations and linguistic applications in which such a recognitional capacity consists, but what *explains* its nature – that is, on what possession and employment of such a capacity is grounded. The answer is: belief in the existence of objects. This is the sense in which having warrant for perceptual assertions, or justification for perceptual judgments, is provided by the conceptual scheme or framework within which they are made, since the scheme is a scheme of persisting spatio-temporal particulars.

It is at this point that the TA to the belief in objects is at work. If perceptual discourse is to be senseful, then we must (that is, it is a necessary condition of the discourse's being senseful) be able to discriminate and individuate items and features in our experience and correlate terms of that discourse with them. It is a necessary condition of our ability to discriminate among and individuate the items over which perceptual discourse ranges, that such items be scrutable, that is, be identifiable and individuable. In order for such items to be identifiable and individuable, it is necessary that they be consistently or systematically so; that is, terms correlated to such items must hold their correlation from one occasion of use to another, and so we must be able to recognise items as those to which a given term properly applies now as on other occasions – which is to say, we must be able to reidentify items. From this point the argument to belief in the existence of objects as a necessary condition of reidentifiability is the same as that given in amplification of Strawson's argument above. Together with the antirelativist argument of Chapter 3, the issue is the demonstration of sceptical doubt as wholly idle. (It is appropriate at this point to remark the similarity between features of this argument about the necessary conditions for the sense of perceptual discourse, and the argument in Chapter 3 about the languagehood criterion; but I shall not expand the point.)

Strawson's argument against the sceptic was earlier characterised as intended to display that, in effect, the proposition 'objects continue to exist unperceived' is entailed by or is otherwise specially related to our conceptual scheme. It is important to understand what this means, for a TA such as the one whose variant expressions have been set out here must, to be satisfactory, yield an account of that intuition. I remarked that this proposition is not to be understood as a claim to the effect that objects are '*really* real' in the absolute sense demanded by the sceptic, which interpretation is ruled out by the fact that the option-B TA employed here is very far from seeking to establish such a conclusion. Rather, it is to be understood as having something like Wittgenstein's 'grammatical' status. 'Grammatical' propositions are those which, Wittgenstein remarks in *On Certainty*, it makes no sense to doubt, and therefore, in an important sense, no sense to assert, or at any rate to claim to 'know'. The most fruitful way to characterise a belief embodied in a proposition of this special kind is to say that it is a *presupposition* of our thinking, talking, and acting as we do, such that to doubt that it *is* a presupposition is not to do something merely false, but senseless. An analogy is provided by the example of the man who prays, attends church, reads devotional literature, is sane, and is neither a dissimulator nor a sociologist conducting a hermeneutic experiment. To doubt or deny that such a man believes in the existence of at least one divinity is to fail to, or to refuse to, understand his practice and whatever assertions he may issue relevant to his practice.

This affords a way of grasping what it means to say that belief in the existence of objects is foundational or basic. Belief in the existence of objects is a necessary condition of the coherence of experience, and so that belief is a presuppositional or foundational belief in the sense that there is no understanding, explaining or characterising experience or what can count as experience without essential reference to the fact that that belief is unquestioningly presupposed by any individual who has or does what can count as having experience. The relation of such a belief to perceptual and general beliefs is then also best characterised as a presupposition or condition of them, an analogy being suggested in this case by the 'covering law' model; for the content of perceptual and general beliefs is as it were governed by, or has the character it does 'in the presence of', the belief that there are objects in the wholly general and fundamental sense presupposed to experience and the talk which reports it. In establishing that this belief is a necessary condition of experience, then, the TA at the same time shows what role it plays. That role is most fruitfully specified as 'foundational', and it is no disadvantage that viewing the foundations of empirical knowledge in these terms is a far cry from the kind of model in which, say, incorrigible sense-data statements alone afford the premisses from which statements about the world are to be inferred. In terms of such a model, in fact, one wishes to say that the *scheme* provides the required supplement for ensuring that sensory experience is logically adequate evidence for, or justification for, ordinary perceptual statements, since the scheme underwrites such judgments, and belief in the existence of objects is foundational with respect to the scheme.

There is something of interest to be learned from looking at different ways of putting the point that belief in the existence of objects is a necessary condition of our thought and talk, chiefly in respect of the verificationist issue raised by Stroud. To say that this belief is necessary to our conceptual scheme is tantamount to saying that realist assumptions are necessary to our conceptual scheme; that, in effect, we are bound to be epistemological (or ontological) realists. Saying 'We are bound to be realists' in this sense is just what is meant by saying that it is a presupposition of experience that it ranges over a realm of objects. But tying the conditions of sense of talk about perceptual experience to a presumption of objects in the way done earlier and above is to make an antirealist point about sense. For grasp of perceptual discourse is tied to knowing the empirical conditions of application for perceptual terms, and being able to recognise that a given set of experiences warrants use of given expressions; sense cannot accrue from experience-transcendent conditions. This demands that there be unquestioning acceptance of belief in the existence of objects as the ground of the capacity to individuate, identify, and reidentify. It is in this sense that to make the point that we must be epistemological realists is to make an antirealist point about sense and the coherence of experience; it exactly parallels Kant's view to the effect that empirical realism is a transcendental idealist thesis. In turn this makes clear how one is to deal with a residual problem, concerning the fact that the foundational belief in question is about *perception-independent* objects of experience. From the viewpoint of the broadly realist tradition in philosophy, talk of 'perception-independence' is taken to be equivalent to talk of 'independence from thought or experience', in the sense that a commitment to talk of the unperceived existence of particulars is taken to entail that such particulars do not in any way depend for their existence on there being any experience or thought whatever. But it can now be seen that there is a difference between perception-independent existence and thought- or experience-independent existence. In a way, one can view Berkeley as having struggled to cope with the experience-dependence of the existence of, say, the quad, and its frequent existential independence of our perceptions of it; and then, failing to recognise the distinction, having to postulate the continuous and universal perceiving of God to bridge the gap. Partly foreshadowed in Hume's naturalistic treatment of discontinuous perception is Kant's solution, to the effect that whereas an object is (to use his terminology) 'nothing to us' unless it is or can be 'thought' by us, none the less part of what it is to be *able* to 'think' an object is to think of it as existing when unperceived. Thus possession of a concept of objects carries with it, as a condition upon the necessary connectedness of experience without which having such a concept would be impossible, the concept's independence of *particular* acts of perceptual awareness of it;[16] but that is far from a claim to the effect that objects are wholly independent of thought or experience in the way that the realist wishes to hold. Here indeed is the difference between the realist and antirealist view of objectivity: the 'absolute' or '*really* real' thesis is the thesis that (a) 'perception-independence of objects' = (b) 'thought-independence of objects', that is, that to say an object exists independently of acts of perceiving entails and is entailed by its existence being independent of all thought and experience in general. This is false, and the distinction between (a) and (b) needs to be kept clearly in view; whereas (b) entails (a), (a) does not entail (b), and

[16] Cf. for example, A104, and Strawson, *Bounds of Sense*, p.73.

that is a fact of great moment.[17]

This thought further strengthens the point made earlier, to the effect that saying we must be epistemological realists is to make an antirealist point. Stroud's view, typifying realist reactions to scepticism, is that scepticism is to be properly defeated only by proving the *truth* of a realist view of the world. The enterprise here, by contrast, shows that scepticism is to be defeated by proving the *necessity of taking* the realist view. The difference is great, not least in that, whereas the former enterprise is unachievable, the latter enterprise is otherwise – as this book consists in showing.

Finally, these antirealist thoughts about experience, and in particular the discourse by which it can be reported, involve bringing the significance or sense of that discourse under empirical constraints, as noted. But these constraints do not amount to a strong verification principle, which at its crudest would have it that propositions are meaningful if and only if they can be known to be true or false. The implausibility of such a principle was quickly enough recognised by early verificationists themselves. To do Stroud credit, he does not exactly characterise in this way the verification principle he purports to discover (looking through realist spectacles) in TAs, but he comes close: his definition is 'concepts are intelligible to us only if we know the empirical conditions under which they could be truly and knowingly applied' (op, cit., p. 114). In any case, Stroud is mistaken about the point at which a verification principle (or rather, an antirealist constraint demanding that there be operative empirical conditions governing the application of terms of perceptual discourse) falls. In Stroud's reconstruction of Strawson's argument, the constraint is made to apply to the issue of reidentification. On the argument of this book, the constraint governs the application of concepts in perception and perceptual discourse, by entering into the minimal conditions of sense for that discourse. If empirical constraints govern sense, they must

[17] This point should not be thought to have Meinongian tendencies; the 'principle of significance' rules that out. Meinong indeed might be regarded as having made a quite opposite mistake; cf. A.C. Grayling, *An Introduction to Philosophical Logic*, Hassocks 1982, chs 2 & 3 (respectively, comments on Meinong; discussion of Lewis, Stalnaker et al. on the 'existence'-'actuality' distinction in possible worlds talk.) See also Grayling, *The Metaphysics of Antirealism*, London, forthcoming, for an extensive treatment of these issues.

themselves, as shown, ultimately depend on empirical beliefs of a certain distinctive character; chiefly, belief in the existence of objects. The TA given here starts with an antirealist characterisation of the sense-conditions for perceptual discourse, and shows that a necessary condition of having the experience which that discourse reports – and *ipso facto* of having that discourse itself – is that the existence of objects be 'unquestioningly accepted' or believed. Stroud's alternative location and strengthening of a thesis about empirical constraints is occasioned by his view – a mistaken one as I have argued – that the TA in question must be an option-A TA, and so must, if it is to be of any use, yield a realist conclusion. On the reformulation and amplification of the TA offered here, the spectre of strong verificationism in the TA itself vanishes.

On this note the project of this essay is completed. If the foregoing discussions are in any way satisfactory, they reveal why sceptical doubt is not in the end troubling: it is because we *have* to believe what we do at the foundations of our conceptual scheme. This is 'the Human shrug'. It is all we either can or need to show, for it shows a great deal.

APPENDIX 1

Empiricism and the *a priori*

A great deal turns upon the notion of basic or transcendental beliefs in the argument of this book. As an heuristic gesture towards the plausibility of making appeal to such beliefs, I wish now to show very briefly that doing so, although clearly a Kantian enterprise, does not despite this mark a radical break with the specifically empirical tradition in pre-Kantian and non-Kantian modern philosophy.

The broadly empiricist tradition since Locke abounds in more or less explicit acknowledgments that there are a priori beliefs, or principles, or features of percipience, which contribute to the organisation of experience. I am concerned to draw attention here to the role which *empiricists* have accorded to a priori features in experience; it is not my concern to cite examples from rationalist epistemology, in which, to characterise it generally and roughly, it is held that by excogitation alone we can attain to wholly certain truths about the universe. There are interesting rationalist thoughts about the role of the a priori in governing 'the appearances', to be sure; but it is central to my argument that the possession and employment of concepts must be tied to empirical conditions of application, and that these turn upon perceptual cues which prompt and govern actual occasions of their application. Accordingly, it is experience, as (in the sense explained) a major part of the 'foundation' of empirical knowledge, which is of interest here, together with the role of a priori features in the organisation of experience so construed. By an a priori concept, belief, or principle I mean, minimally, one not acquired as a result of empirical observation; this is not to say that the conditions of applicability for at least some a priori concepts are non-empirical.[1]

[1] Cf. A.C. Grayling, op. cit. ch. 3 passim.

Kant, and writers like Strawson and Ross Harrison, hold the kind of views with which I wish to compare certain features of the empirical tradition. Kant made central use of the idea that there are a priori features in experience, which we as cognitive agents contribute to the organisation of the inflow of intuition. Indeed, because in his view space, time, and the categories are 'a priori conditions of the possibility of experience' (*CPR* A94/B126), these features do more than merely organise experience; without them experience would be impossible. Recent work by Strawson and Ross Harrison is similar in spirit but less swingeing in the extent of its claims about the basic necessities for experience. Strawson argued that having satisfiable criteria for the reidentification of particulars is one of the conditions for the coherence of experience, and that having such criteria demands the continued independent existence of particulars (*Individuals*, pp. 33ff.), and in a detailed discussion of Kant he defended, with some reworking, the latter's view that apperception is fundamental to coherent experience and is itself possible only on condition that we have applicable concepts of the objective (*Bounds of Sense*, pp. 97-112). Harrison described his enterprise as 'an enquiry into the essential features of any comprehensible world';[2] his first and most basic premiss is that reasons must be available to 'the protagonist' enabling him to distinguish among the judgments he makes as to which are true and which false, and he argues that it is a condition of this that 'the world must be connected together so that the truth of some judgments could form reasons for the truth or falsity of others' (pp. 51ff.). In Kant and some recent writers of this persuasion, transcendental arguments play a crucial role. Despite sometimes wide differences of approach, terminology, and detail, the spirit of the enterprise is the same throughout; the idea is that our conceptual scheme contains features which are fundamental and pervasive, and which in some sense make experience possible. I shall for convenience call this the 'Kantian insight'.

In the work of a number of philosophers who are either not Kantian or who predate Kant, there are notions which come close to the Kantian insight or echo it. In Kant and the recent writers mentioned, a strong point is being argued for; that a priori features in experience are necessary to experience. By contrast, a weaker point is

[2] R. Harrison, *On What There Must Be*, Oxford 1974, p. 207.

made by others in the modern tradition, to the effect that there is a degree of a priori contribution to the organisation of experience; but they do not go so far as to suggest that this contribution consists in *necessary* structural features of our thought about the world. The philosophers I have it in mind to cite are Locke, Hume, Russell, and Mackie. Of these, only Hume seems to have been unaware that some extension of his views along the lines later adopted by Kant would have been fruitful; it was indeed Kant, who in response to Hume, recognised what manoeuvre was required in order to attempt solution of the difficulties confronting Hume. In making this manoeuvre, Kant went – as one might say – the whole hog. With regard to the others it seems to be that caution, perhaps undue, prevailed.

The thoughts of both Locke and Mackie in this connection are complicated by the fact that they associate the matter of a priori contributions to experience with the controversy over innate ideas. Locke was programmatically committed to the view that the mind commences as a *tabula rasa* which is written upon by experience; Mackie, in considering the issue of innate ideas and Lockean empiricism,[3] felt obliged, as against Locke, to make concessions to innatist doctrine in order to allow for us to be realists. Tying the question of what the mind contributes in experience to the question of innate ideas is a mistake, for it confuses questions of the genesis of concepts with questions concerning the conditions of their applicability and the order of logical dependence between them. It is probably right to say, and my discussion in the body of the book strongly implies this, that we learn our conceptual scheme by learning a language; but saying *how* we come by our scheme or certain of its constituent concepts does little to give us a proper account of it. Bearing in mind the obscuring provenance of Locke's and Mackie's views in this connection, then, their thoughts are something as follows.

Locke says that the mind is 'fitted to receive impressions' (*Essay* II.i.§24) in virtue of 'natural tendencies imprinted' upon it (I.iii.§3). Awareness of the acts and contents of consciousness accompany all perceptions; the mind 'attends to' its ideas of perception and reflection, and performs upon them operations of association,

[3] J.L. Mackie, *Problems from Locke*, Oxford 1976, ch. 7 passim.

combination, abstraction, and so forth. Ideas of unity, existence, substance, infinity, power and cause are not given rise to in sensation, but are explanatory or organisational ideas which the mind uses to structure experience. Ideas of unity and existence associate with 'every object without, and every idea within' (II.vii.§9); the idea of substance is an idea with no correlate in sensation but which collects bundles of qualities[4] and cannot be dispensed with – it is a 'supposition' about the support of existing qualities 'which we imagine cannot subsist *sine re substante*' (II.xxiii.§2). Locke is far from holding that the mind is wholly passive in sensation; its contribution is such that in perception the ideas received by sensation are 'altered by judgment, without our taking note of it' (II.ix.§8).

It seemed to Locke important to explain the derivation of these organising ideas, because he was defending a stringent empiricism and was hostile to the notion that any idea whatever, even these, could be *antecedent* to experience although not derived from it. Accordingly he located the origins of these ideas in reflection. The mind notices recurring features of perceptions, and generalises from them to form complex ideas of the organisational kind listed. Mackie found this manoeuvre implausible because in his view it does not afford latitude for the realism he wishes to reconcile with empiricism.[5] To make room for realism, Mackie says that 'further extensions' are needed to empiricism (p. 211). The extensions – cautiously made, to be sure – consist in holding that our 'seeing things realistically', our having concepts of substance, identity and causality, our placing reliance on inductive reasoning and our holding to some form of the principle of the uniformity of nature, might be, or be encouraged by, innate propensities to perceive and think in these terms. Mackie is anxious to make as minimal a claim as possible, talking of the possible possession of innate presumptions of objectivity as 'an inborn reluctance to interpret what (one) sees as disorderly sequences' (p. 222).

It is not easy to see how Locke squares the mind's fitness to treat of impressions with its being a *tabula rasa*. Leibniz's metaphor of the mind as grained marble, suitably understood, would seem to suit

[4] Cf. First letter to Dr Stillingfleet.

[5] This forms a large part of Mackie's enterprise in *Problems from Locke*: cf. pp. 3-4.

Locke's purposes better. Mackie carefully discriminates his own view of our realist propensities from Leibniz's more extensive commitment to the idea that, in addition to having innate preferences among empirical beliefs, we also, and more importantly, have actual and certain knowledge of necessary truths over a wide range – in arithmetic, geometry, logic, theology and ethics. For Mackie, 'authorative, autonomous knowledge' has as a requirement 'independent empirical confirmation' (ibid). He dismisses the idea that we have knowledge of necessary truths.

Presumably therefore Mackie would hold that our presumption against disorder is, although in a sense innate, a contingent matter; for he holds that it is merely in virtue of limitations upon our powers of imagination that we cannot conceive of experience without the organising concepts listed, and that these therefore are not *necessary* features of our conceptual scheme.[6] But the consequence of this is that the explanatory value of appealing to these particular innate concepts is much diminished, for if we could think about the world in ways which do not at all involve these concepts, then we learn nothing definitive about the world by inspecting these concepts, and therefore it is difficult to see how they can be concepts the fact of our possession of which defends *realism.* Mackie's realism is a thesis to the effect that there are entities of certain kinds whose existence is in no way dependent upon our experience of them. On his view, realism results from its being the best and simplest hypothesis available to account for our experience. This raises the difficulty mentioned: if there are other kinds of concepts basic (on Mackie's own admission) to the kind of experience we *do* in fact have, what price realism?

At any rate, what is important for present purposes is that both Locke and Mackie explicitly hold that there are a priori elements in the organisation of experience. Neither, of course, accords them the status they assume in Kant's enterprise.

Hume's admission to the same effect is implicit; perhaps it is better described as one made by default. No idea is perspicuous or perfectly intelligible, Hume held, unless it can be traced to its origin in the 'primary impression, from which it arises' (*Treatise*, ed. Selby-Bigge, pp. 74-5). This is the methodological principle Hume employed in doing for human nature what Newton did for inanimate nature – i.e.

[6] Mackie, *Cement of the Universe*, ch. 4 passim: cf. pp. 96ff.

giving a wholly general account of it based on a few fundamental principles. Now, perceiving for Hume is 'a mere passive admission of the impression thro' the organs of sense' (p. 73), but of course much of what is important in human life is not restricted to the present contents of conciousness, but involves belief in 'matters of fact, beyond the present testimony of our senses' (*Enquiry*, ed. Selby-Bigge, p. 26). In order to have such beliefs, we must make inferences to them; otherwise 'we should never know how to adjust means to ends ... there would be an end at once of all action, as well as of the chief part of speculation' (p. 45). It is therefore crucial for human thought and action that we are able to order our view of things beyond the immediately present data of sense. For Hume, all inferences from what is observed to what is unobserved are *causal* inferences, are 'reasonings ... founded on the relation of *Cause and Effect*' (p. 26). Causation, together with resemblance and contiguity, constitute 'the only ties of our thoughts, they are really *to us* the cement of the universe, and all the operations of the mind must, in a great measure, depend on them' (Hume's *Abstract*). And Hume of course held that belief in the independent existence of physical objects plays the same role, that is, that it is likewise crucial to human thought and action (*Treatise*, p. 189).

The account Hume gives of causation and 'the existence of bodies' is therefore on his own view central. It is not to my purpose here to report his arguments on these matters, but to focus on his conclusions. These are notorious. Causal nexuses are distinguished from non-causal ones, says Hume, by a relation of necessary connection between causes and effects; yet the idea of necessary connection does not arise from impressions or reason, but is supplied by 'custom' or 'imagination', or certain 'natural' or 'primitive' dispositions of the mind (pp. 153-60). (Stroud, in his book on Hume, aptly heads his discussion of this issue with the couplet 'Great Standing Miracle! That Heav'n assigned/Its only thinking thing this turn of mind)'. The same goes for 'bodies'. Our believing in the continued and distinct existence of bodies is something we simply *do*; we have no choice in the matter; our belief in them 'is an affair of too great importance to be entrusted to our uncertain reasonings and speculations' (*Treatise*, p. 238). It is, he says, 'vain to ask *whether* there be body or not. That is a point which we must take for granted in all our reasonings' (pp. 245-6). We do not derive the notions of continued distinct physical existence from either impressions or reason; it is once again a matter of custom, an integral feature of our thought which is best secured, so far as philosophical doubt is concerned, by 'inattention', and which is given rise to by the 'constancy and coherence' imputed to the impressions of objects by the mind (*Treatise*, p. 243).

Causality and objectivity are therefore fundamental to human thought and action, but our notions of them arise neither from experience nor reason, but are contributed by the 'imagination' as, in the case of causality, a 'tie of our thoughts' and, in the case of objectivity, something 'we *must* take for granted' in all our reasonings. Hume did not go further; he did not ask, as Kant did, whether these observations yield an extremely important further clue about what sort of account should be given of the nature of our thought. As I see it, these features of Hume's views together with those in Locke and Mackie of the same tendency, render yet more plausible the spirit – at least – of Kant's enterprise.

Russell might appear an unlikely candidate for inclusion here, not least because of his strictures on placing human experience at the centre of things, and the scorn he reserved for Kant's 'Ptolemaic counter-revolution' to this effect.[7] Despite this, Russell felt unable to achieve *some* measure of security for human knowledge against scepticism[8] without offering and defending certain 'postulates' which must be true if inductive inferences are validly to yield us scientific knowledge, which knowledge he takes for granted.[9] This is a highly interesting manoeuvre for Russell to have made.

Hume's point about what, if any, license we have for moving from the observed to the unobserved – the problem of induction – exercised Russell greatly, and he made a number of attempts to deal with it. The problem can be put generally by asking whether there are any inductive propositions someone S is rational in believing, such propositions being inductive for S if at a time *t* the content of the propositions constitutes some evidence for, and is consistent with but

[7] B. Russell, *Human Knowledge: its scope and limits,* London 1948, p. 9.

[8] He did not think *total* security against scepticism possible, but believed we could have good reason not to be sceptical; cf. *My Philosophical Development*, pp. 207.

[9] *Human Knowledge*, p. 524.

at least partly outside the content of, S's experience at *t*.[10] What is required is the identification of some characteristic of inductive inferences which, as Sainsbury puts it, we intuitively recognise as 'strong', such that this characteristic attaches to all and only such inferences and helps us to discriminate between them, on the one hand, and intuitively implausible or 'weak' inferences on the other. Thus (a) 'The sun has risen every day in my experience, so it will rise tomorrow' is an intuitively strong inductive inference which we would expect to find manifests the desired characteristic, while (b) 'The sun has risen every day in my experience, so it will not rise tomorrow' is intuitively a weak inductive inference whose weakness we would expect to find explained by the absence of the desired characteristic (Sainsbury, ibid.). The effect of strong arguments by Russell and Goodman in this connection was to diminish the plausibility of invoking an assumption of the uniformity of nature to serve as that feature which yields or embodies the desired characteristic.[11]

Against the background of this problem – together with his resolve to regard science as true and then discover what must be the case given that it is true – Russell put to work an application of his view that: 'Since inferences start from premises, there must be knowledge which is uninferred if there is to be any knowledge' (*Human Knowledge*, p. 181). In the case of the postulates which must be true because science is true, they are more than just uninferred, they are a priori: 'Either ... we know something independently of experience, or science is moonshine' (p. 175). Science is not moonshine, therefore we know something a priori; what we know a priori turns a strong inductive argument into a valid inductive argument when added to its premisses.

The postulates have impressed very few critics, for such reasons as that if science admits of empirical refutation, which Russell would acknowledge it does, then the status of the postulates is highly questionable. Russell regarded them as contingent, although a priori, and therefore vulnerable to standing or falling with science; yet otherwise Russell's understanding of 'a priori' is the traditional one to the effect that anything knowable a priori is necessary, and

[10] Cf. R. Sainsbury, *Russell*, London 1979, p. 164.

[11] Russell 'On the notion of cause' in *Mysticism and Logic*, London 1956, pp. 14ff.; Nelson Goodman, *Fact, Fiction, and Forecast*, London 1954, p. 74.

that only experience can tell us how things in fact are (cf. pp. 211-17). His general accounts of a priori knowledge as such are slim and unconvincing, so there are few materials to hand for constructing a satisfactory defence of these views.

It is not in my view the case that Russell was mistaken in thinking that something like the postulates are grounding conditions for the validity of scientific thought, because it is just my position that something like these postulates, and the role they have in validating our beliefs about the world, are fundamental to our having empirical beliefs at all. The difficulties in Russell's account arise from whether the postulates accord with other of Russell's views, and in particular what status, given those other views, they are meant to have. However, it is not my concern to criticise or defend Russell here, but merely to point out the fact that he felt impelled to adopt the strategy of invoking a priori features in the organisation of experience, a temptation strongly felt and apparent in the work of the non- or pre-Kantians already cited.

It is important for my purpose to ask a question which naturally arises as a result of the preceding sketches. Given that these philosophers acknowledged important a priori elements in the organisation of experience, why did they not go as far as Kant in accepting them as necessary features of our conceptual scheme? The answer, I think, reveals the respect in which these philosophers, and by extension the broad tradition in which they are central figures, were most profoundly mistaken in their approach. The mistake, as it seems to me, is radical and in very large measure vitiates their enterprise. It is that they assumed that *showing where our ideas came from* is somehow much the greatest part of what is needed to give a satisfactory account of human knowledge; that revealing the origin of our ideas comes to the same thing as justifying our beliefs about the world, as though one cannot give an account of the justificatory structure of our beliefs without tying it to the question of their psychogenetic history. It is common to all these philosophers that much attention is paid to the issue of how our ideas are originally derived; and it is precisely for the reason that they were committed to attempting to prove the origin of knowledge in sense experience, that the uncomfortable presence of a priori features in the organisation of that experience is dealt with by them in an uncertain, fumbling, and often off-hand way.

On bare inspection, the notion that the way to give a justifying account of knowledge is to show where as a matter of psychological history our ideas are derived from is startling and puzzling. Suppose we could show in this way that *all* our ideas are derived from experience. What does this prove? Taking myself to experience bodies does not entail that there are bodies, and therefore does not without supplement justify my belief in their existence; having simple ideas of qualities like redness does not entail that there is any red thing independent of my having a red sense-datum, and therefore does not of itself justify me in believing there are things which are red other than my sense-data. Notoriously, the sceptical doubts about what if any justification we can have for these or those beliefs is settled neither by the mere fact that we have them, nor by showing that experience is a necessary condition of our having them. The argument presumably is that there are ways of getting ideas which somehow make those ideas more secure, that is, epistemically more privileged, than if they had been acquired in other ways; this on analogy with the fact that if a surgeon tells me how to perform a caesarian section, then his account is preferable to the instruction on the same head provided by a tailor or an accountant. The empiricists' insistence on *experience* as the *source* of our ideas arises from what they take to be the fact that we are most directly and surely acquainted with the immediate objects of experience (that is, our sensings) than with whatever can be inferred from them; but it is a major problem to settle what can be meant by direct acquaintance, given the difficulties over such issues as theory-ladenness and 'the given'.

These issues aside, and concentrating only on the general empiricist point (that is, that showing where ideas originate goes the greatest part of the way to justifying our possession of them), it is surely relevant to point out that in general it is the merest prejudice to *begin* by saying that unless a given idea can be traced to such-and-such a source, we are not warranted in holding it. If one asks, what does it explain, justify, or prove to show what the source of our ideas is? and the answer is, it shows how we are justified in placing epistemological reliance upon them, then this answer is only satisfactory if it is also true, or assumed to be true, that there is a particular source of our ideas somehow better than others from the point of view of conferring epistemic warrant on them; but this latter cannot be shown, at least at the outset of giving an account of knowledge, for the reason that there are no independent reasons why one rather than another source of ideas *should* – again, at the outset – be chosen as epistemologically privileged.

Moreover, the 'genetic presumption', as it might be called, is extraordinarily misleading as employed by members of this tradition. It is not the case, as at its crudest the tradition implies, that individuals do or could construct the world *ab ovo* by inference from their sensory experiences. Arguably, no individual learns anything from his sensory experience which is not an extension to, or reclassification of the elements in, whatever corpus of beliefs about the world he so far has. This claim might seem improbable in connection with, say, infants; but here, at best, it can be contested only by means of a wrangle over when it is appropriate to impute beliefs to conscious beings. An infant in the first weeks of life will recoil from an object advanced rapidly towards his face, or shut his eyes quickly upon feeling an unexpected touch in their vicinity. A reflex is not a belief; although when an adult on uncertain footing performs some such (reflex) action as shooting out his arms to keep balance, the fact that he is aware of what he is doing and can give an account of it, inclines us to say that he has at very least dispositional beliefs about the world relevant to his situation. From the viewpoint of armchair psychology, we can say that the infant's reflex activities are appropriate to his environmental conditions, and that he will later come to be aware of them and to articulate them. There can be no question of *inference* to the objective relata in transactions which make him dodge and blink; they are 'given' in the sense of being already as much part of the world's furniture as his mother's breast on day one. Like the rest of us he will learn to classify and extend this furniture as he acquires a command of a language embodying classifications and a myriad hypostatisation of the possible objects of experience; if he becomes a philosopher or scientist he may effect some reclassification or additions for the benefit and enlightenment of mankind. However, this genetic (more accurately, psychogenetic) account of the origin of an individual's beliefs tells us very little about the structure, and far less about the justification, of the beliefs he holds, which is a *philosophical* issue and not a *psychological* one. No more does the genetic account of the Lockean tradition, with its experiencing subject putatively constructing the world – or at least able in principle to construct the world – out of his sensory ideas.

It is worth considering further the view that if it were shown how an individual *could* in principle construct the world from his sense-experience, then the justification of our beliefs is secured. Putting matters this way retains the prejudice that the mere fact of their originating in sense-experience warrants our beliefs; but it does have the virtue of showing more clearly that the intention of the exercise is to give an account of the *structure* of our belief-system. It is after all the issue of justification which is crucial, and this way of handling the matter is designed to show that our ordinary common-sense beliefs can be shown to stem from something direct and therefore self-justifying, or at least more direct and therefore more largely self-justifying, than those common-sense beliefs themselves. But why should it be supposed at the outset that tracing the justification chain to sense-experience settles the issues better than tracing them to, say, the generosity of an honest divinity? It is owing to the *programme* of empiricist philosophy, to the effect that experience is (all but alone) sufficient for knowledge, that empiricists feel uncomfortable about the status of a priori features in knowledge. In Kant and some recent writers, the question of the source of our ideas – of how we came by them – is very much less important than the question how, given that we have the ideas we do, we can show what the structure of our common-sense view of the world is and why it is justified. For Kant and these others, the issue of the empirical conditions for the applicability of concepts ('concepts without intuitions are blind') is of central and obvious importance, and this secures to experience a central role in talk of knowledge; whereas for those in the tradition stemming from Locke, the very different matter of the experiential *origin* of ideas is what is thought to be of importance, and this, as it seems to me, is a great deal less satisfactory, not least in view of the fact that Locke and his successors are at once forced to acknowledge and yet, in consequence of their programme, to fudge the matter of a priori elements in our world-view, and the role they play in producing it.

It is instructive to note that a recent attempt, owing to Ayer, to construct the world from experience throws into sharp relief the indispensability of the kind of notions upon which Kant and the

Kantian tradition focus so much attention.[12] In showing how our common-sense interpretation of our experience is founded upon that experience (p. 91), Ayer *begins* by assuming as given to an observer the following: colour qualia with size and shape, in sets of patterns between which spatial and temporal relations hold, all of which the observer can record when they occur (p. 95). Because the observer 'can make no progress so long as we confine his attention to the contents of a single visual field' (p. 99) he must be credited with memories and expectations, so that he can locate the patterns of qualia he recognises in an extended spatio-temporal continuum (p. 99-100). Moreover, there is 'an important empirical fact, without which, indeed, the development of our theory would not be possible', and it is 'that the observer inhabits a predominantly stable world' (p. 100). So far, beyond the mere appearance to the observer of colour qualia, the observer is said to have at the outset certain abilities and concepts *as givens*; namely the ability to perceive qualia as patterned, and to discriminate between patterns (i.e. to have criteria of identity sufficient to know when one pattern stops and another begins), primitive concepts of space and time, criteria for recognising similarities and making comparisons across space and time (i.e. comparative, identifying and reidentifying criteria), and a presumption of coherence and orderliness in his experience (Ayer says a presumption of order in the world, but the world has not yet arrived). On condition that the observer is thus equipped, he can derive the notion of the persistence of percepts, and movement; then he proceeds to a Humean awareness of himself as a body, that is, as a percept or set of percepts different from the rest of his percepts (p. 102); and having done so he is able to distinguish between his own experience and the things he perceives, the great majority of which latter he by now interprets objectively (p. 104). From this point onwards Robinson Crusoe can go no further in constructing the world without a Man Friday to assist him, because the experience and judgments of others come at this point into important focus (pp. 104-5).

In giving this account Ayer was not setting out to show how, as a matter of psychological-historical fact, any individual constructs the world; but, rather, his concern was to mark, by means of an analytic

[12] A.J. Ayer, *The Central Questions of Philosophy*, pp. 91-106.

reconstruction, 'the general features of our experience that make it possible for each of us to employ the theory successfully' (p. 106). This is not at all far removed from the spirit of a Kantian approach to the problem even though Ayer characterises this strategy as similar to Hume's. The *difference* between Ayer's project and Hume's, in fact, is the very difference made by Kant. Certainly there are features of Ayer's account, notably the place occupied by the self, which differ widely from the Kantian role that the self would play in this kind of approach; but it is not so much matters of detail as matters of programme which it is of interest to pick out here. In Ayer's later thought on the topic, then, he moved from a point in the broadly Lockean tradition to a point close to the concerns of the broadly Kantian tradition, which movement, it seems to me, speaks volumes as to the rival merits of each in furnishing materials for a satisfactory epistemology.

The aim in this Appendix has been to defend the plausibility, in a general way, of placing weight on the notion of there being a priori concepts fundamental to the coherence of our conceptual scheme. The idea that there are such concepts is a Kantian one, but I have sketched here how certain non-Kantian philosophers from Locke to Mackie made appeal, and felt themselves obliged to make appeal, to concepts of this kind, although they attempted to place as little weight upon them as possible owing to their desire to view experience-derived ideas as, alone, the really important ones. It is the fact that these philosophers were obliged to acknowledge a priori elements in the organisation of experience which suggests that it is plausible and valuable to do as Kant did, namely to look to them for help in giving a proper account of our common-sense beliefs and claims about the world. In showing, throughout the main body of the book, how particular knowledge claims are justified, I make use of the notion that there are a priori concepts which are fundamental to experience; in formulating transcendental arguments I attempt to give one of these a priori concepts its own justification. Accordingly these a priori concepts, or 'transcendental beliefs' as I give reason for calling them, play a crucial role in the argument.

APPENDIX 2

Knowledge, belief and beliefs

Because two separable though related concerns govern contemporary epistemology, it needs to be made quite clear just what epistemological issue is being tackled in the main body of this book, and where in the range of contemporary epistemological concerns it lies. This will also allow me to comment briefly on the question of the nature of belief as understood in the body of this book.

The two related but separable concerns of contemporary epistemology are (1) the problem of stating necessary and sufficient conditions for its being true that someone knows that *p*, and (2) the problem of showing how, if at all, we are justified in believing what we do. This latter concern is the more traditional and fundamental of the two, and it is in connection with it that scepticism arises. Indeed it is appropriate to say that it is scepticism which motivates our interest in this problem by purporting to show that what we ordinarily take ourselves to be justified in asserting of the external world is not justified. It is to issue (2) that I address myself in this book, and not (1).

The relation and the difference between the two concerns of contemporary epistemology can be characterised in this way. The problem of stating the conditions for knowledge was thrown into prominence by Gettier's defeating counterexamples to the standard analysis of knowledge as justified true belief.[1] Gettier showed that a person can make an apparently proper inference from a belief he is justified in holding, but which is false, to a belief which is true but whose truth is unrelated to the premisses it was inferred from. More general examples have been constructed to the same end of showing that the standard analysis of knowledge is insufficient owing to

[1] E. Gettier, 'Is justified true belief knowledge?', *Analysis*, 23 (1963), pp. 121-3.

difficulties infecting an appropriate specification of the kind of justification needed for the belief to constitute knowledge. Among the strategies suggested to ensure a satisfactory analysis have been that a belief amounts to knowledge if its justification does not proceed by way of any falsehoods, or if the reasons *S* has for *P* are 'conclusive' reasons, or if the justification for the belief in question is indefeasible.

What is assumed in discussion of this kind is that beliefs can be justified; the problem in (1) is not to defend in general the notion that epistemic beliefs can be justified, but to show when justified belief amounts to knowledge. The issue of epistemic justification itself, problem (2), is prior to this, and more fundamental; for if scepticism about the justification of our beliefs cannot be defeated, then we do not have justified beliefs, and therefore the question cannot arise as to when these (or, which of these) justified beliefs constitute knowledge. It is the question whether in general beliefs can be justified, and therefore the question how sceptical doubt about such justification can be defused, which is crucial and which I tackle here.

Sometimes scepticism is represented as a demonstration that, given some definition of 'knowledge', no justified belief can amount to knowledge. This scepticism Williams characterises as no more than a 'carping about the use of the verb "to know" '.[2] It is of course interesting and important to get a precise specification of the concept of knowledge in terms of an account of when or which justified beliefs amount to it, but it is no major matter that, because these or those strict conditions for knowledge have been added – for example, that it be 'certain' or 'totally secure', etc. – life has been made more difficult for epistemologists devoted to an analysis of the concept of knowledge *per se*. This hardly amounts to scepticism; such a 'sceptic' might define 'knowledge' out of reach, and yet hold that we are justified in all our ordinary beliefs. Much more damaging is scepticism which says: the pressing question is whether we are ever justified in holding the beliefs we do hold about the external world, for there are these and those reasons which suggest that we are not justified in believing what we do. *This* problem, to repeat, is my concern here: I am not concerned to specify the necessary and

[2] M. Williams, *Groundless Belief*, London 1977, p. 4.

sufficient conditions which would have to be satisfied for a justified belief to count as knowledge.

In view of this, there is little reason not to use such expressions as 'know that *p*' and 'knowledge claims', meaning by such usage no more than is normally comprehended in colloquial and intuitive uses of 'know' and 'knowledge', and on the whole meaning by this 'justified belief' where this latter expression is not qualified in some way as to render the belief in question of lesser epistemic status than would intuitively qualify it to count as knowledge-adequate belief. This is not intended, again, to presuppose or promise some solution to the question of the analysis of knowledge as such, that is, to the question of the conditions for the truth of 'S knows that P'.

One useful purpose which would be served by retaining 'know' and 'knowledge' in this intuitive sense would be that it avoids certain ambiguities which infect 'believe' and 'belief' as follows: we sometimes say that someone '*only*' (or '*merely*') believes *p*, meaning that S *himself* would not claim to *know p* 'for sure', i.e. believe *p* in the strong 'knowledge adequate' sense of being well justified in believing *p* true. Descartes sitting by the fire in his dressing gown and holding a piece of paper *believes* that he is sitting thus, but the sceptical doubts he raises (he might, he says, be dreaming) throw question on whether he *knows* it. This is not a cavil about 'know', but a question about justification. There would be no sense in being sceptical about something one did not at all believe; I do not in any sense now believe that I am lying on a beach somewhere in the Bahamas, so the question 'Ah! but are you *really* lying on a beach somewhere in the Bahamas'? is pointless. However, I believe I am sitting up at a desk somewhere in Oxford, so the same question, with suitable revisions in its postural and geographical aspects, takes on point. Of Descartes' case it can be said that he (merely) believes that he is sitting etc., but the sceptical doubt is – is he justified in taking it that he is? It is to mark the difference between the mere and the strong senses of 'belief', as here characterised, that one would be justified in retaining the colloquial use of 'know' to capture the strong sense. Having made this point about 'believes', however, I talk in the main body of the book of belief rather than knowledge since it is strictly more correct to do so.

A question naturally arises concerning what is to be understood by 'belief'. The ambiguity just sketched is not the only one, for there is the further complication that 'belief' can signify a state of mind (contrasted with 'disbelief'), and also the object of the propositional attitude in which that state of mind consists – '*a* or *the* belief that *p*'. We have a good intuitive grasp of what it is to believe that *p*, and what *p*s – the beliefs believed – can variously be. In a focal case such as belief about the way things are in the world, one would say, minimally, that if S believes *p* then S is prepared in the relevant circumstances to assert, or to act on the strength of, *p*; or to assert or to act on the strength of *q* or *r* where *p* entails, supports, or even just, in some cases, suggests that they are the case. This is tantamount to saying that S takes *p* to be true or more likely to be true than competitors to *p*; so that it is appropriate to characterise believing as 'taking to be true or most likely to be true'. For the reasons set out in Chapter 2 it is useful to dispense with an appeal to truth in this connection, and to substitute 'S's believing *p* consists in S's regarding himself or anyone else as warranted in asserting and/or acting upon *p*, or more strongly warranted in asserting and/or acting upon *p* than any competitor to *p*'.

A belief as the object of the propositional attitude sketched would then be most usefully characterised as what is, in the focal case, statable in the form 'Things are thus and so', and this also *as a reason* for S's acting in a certain way, or for asserting *p* or any *q* or *r* suitably related to *p*. Recognising that S holds a certain belief therefore at least rests upon observing that S is disposed to speak and act in ways which would be unintelligible unless one accorded possession of the relevant belief to him. Thus if S in all seriousness and earnestness prays, goes to church, reads religious literature, is not a sociologist, and is otherwise sane, it would be appropriate to ascribe to him belief in the existence of at least one divinity.

People can believe what is impossible, false, unwarranted, or unwise; and monkeys can (at least not inappropriately, be said to) believe what is possible, true, warranted, or prudent. These facts raise two rather different further features of belief. The first is relatively unproblematic; believing is a broader and more liberal propositional attitude than knowing is supposed to be, since knowing *p* is standardly taken to entail the truth of *p*. The question of non-language-possessing creatures having beliefs is slightly more complicated. The problem here is the same as the problem of ascribing possession of concepts in general to such creatures, and I deal with that in Chapter 3.

Sketching matters in this way amounts to resisting the notion that talk of beliefs and believing is not philosophically perspicuous. I use the term 'belief' in the main body of the argument to do duty for the propositional act and the object both, the context making it clear which is meant; and unless there are attendant qualifications, I mean no more or less by the term than here characterised.

APPENDIX 3

The justification regress and foundationalism

The matter of epistemic justification has two aspects. There is the question (1) What is it for a belief, or set of beliefs, to justify another belief? And there is the question (2) Is there a justification regress, and if so does it terminate; if it does, where, and if it does not, how is it that beliefs can be said to be justified ultimately – or do we anyway need to say such a thing? The sceptical problem relates to both these issues, and both have to be dealt with if the problem scepticism poses is to be resolved. However, there are certain considerations relating to the second of these questions which it would be particularly useful to raise here.

Given an understanding of the justification relation (or relations, for there may be more than one) the question of a justification regress arises. Whatever else it is, a justification relation between a justifying belief and the belief it justifies will normally consist in an inference from the former, as constituting the required kind of evidence for belief in the latter, to that latter; and moreover, it must be at least part of the condition for some belief or set of beliefs *e* to be a justification for someone S's believing *p* (at *t*), that *e* itself be justified or justifiable for S (at *t*) whether *e* is in some sense a self-justified belief (if there are any such) or whether it is justified in its own turn by inference from prior (either inferentially justified or self-justified) beliefs.[1] It is of course manifest that many of our beliefs are not immediately justified by inference from beliefs which are in some sense self-justified or non-inferentially justified, if there are any; and for this reason we are faced with the issue of a justification regress.

The next question is therefore whether the regress has a terminus in basic, i.e. self-justified or non-inferentially justified, beliefs, or whether it proceeds either in regress *ad infinitum* or in a circle. Views to the effect that the regress has a terminus in basic beliefs are generally called foundationalist views; until latterly these have been the main kind of views in this field, but non-foundationalist theories, particularly 'coherence' theories of knowledge, are currently in vogue, chiefly because the difficulties which are seen to infect foundationalist views are claimed by their critics and commentators to constitute warrant for abandoning foundationalism altogether.[2]

The argument of this book is, on a rough characterisation, foundationalist in spirit, and it is therefore instructive from the point of view of my concerns here to look briefly at some of the options and difficulties of foundationalism in general. This will allow the identification of certain very general desiderata for any foundationalist theory which is to be successful, and these may be used to test the views urged here.

In general, an epistemological theory of justification is foundationalist in character if it holds (a) that there is a class of beliefs B such that every member of B is in some sense self-justified and/or non-inferential, and (b) such that for any justified belief p, if p is not a member of B then either it is justified by direct inference from B or from an inferential series of justified beliefs $p_1 \dots p_n$ with a terminal member which is a member of B. For a theory to be non-foundationalist in character it is sufficient that it rest upon the contrary of (b); it does not have to rest upon the contrary of (a). It is for this reason that not all non-foundationalist theories have to be coherence theories.[3]

[1] Justification need not always proceed in terms of beliefs. For example, my belief that something is a certain colour may not be based on my belief that it looks that colour to me, but simply on its looking that colour to me.

[2] Cf. J.W. Cornman, *Materialism and Sensations*, New York 1971, Pt. III; M. Williams, op. cit.; K. Lehrer, *Knowledge*, Oxford 1974.

[3] Cf. Cornman, op. cit.

The first matter of importance is that the members of B should be properly specified. Critics of foundationalism have concentrated most attention on this issue. Candidates for basic beliefs have varied in kind from beliefs about one's immediate sense-data to specified ranges of beliefs about current perceptual environments; and, in addition, views on the required strength of self-justification for such beliefs have varied widely from a strong requirement of incorrigibility to modest self-warrant relative to someone at a time. These options, of course, lie within the range of theories which assume, as do I, that there are empirical conditions operative with respect to the question of the validity of beliefs, which are crucial to any account of justification; it may be part of the foundationalist story for Descartes or Berkeley that some if not all our beliefs are wholly warranted in virtue of being secured by God, but, granting that it is logically possible that this is true, I shall not take account of it here, nor of any doctrine which dispenses with central use of a notion of *empirical content*, in some sense of this phrase, in the justification conditions for beliefs.

Satisfactory specification of the members of B involves showing how they themselves are justified, keeping in view the requirement that, as the termini of justification chains, they cannot themselves be inferred from yet more basic beliefs, and must somehow be self-justified. In addition to stating principles of justification for basic beliefs, it needs to be shown satisfactorily how justification is transmitted from them to the inferentially justified beliefs based upon them. Accordingly two classes of justification principles are required: one relevant to the justification of basic beliefs, and one relevant to the transmission of justification through the belief-corpus based on them. Nothing rules out in advance that there will be just two principles, one for each of these two broad levels of justified beliefs; thus transmission principles may include deduction, suitably construed inductive procedures, 'criterial' relations and/or other connecting principles yet to be specified. That this may well be so is suggested by the obvious facts that (a) until basic beliefs are characterised, it cannot be settled what kinds of relations they can bear to non-basic beliefs, and (b) the notion of diferent strengths of justification for non-basic beliefs may be interpretable just in terms of the different transmission principles yielding them.

Because non-foundationalist theories share with foundationalist theories the problem of giving an account of transmission principles, critics of foundationalism have concentrated their attack upon the principles of justification for basic beliefs. Showing that the difficulty of giving a satisfactory account of these is insuperable would entail by elimination that non-foundationalist approaches to epistemology are correct. Criticism has taken this form:[4] for *any* belief *b*, if it is justified for someone S then he must have some *reason* for thinking it true (or likely to be true). Such a reason must consist in S's having justified beliefs to the effect that if any belief has some property or feature φ it is true (or likely to be true). Such a reason must consist in S's having justified beliefs to the effect that if any belief has some property or feature φ it is true (or likely to be true), and that *b* has φ. But then if this is how any b is justified for S, then no *b* can be a basic belief, because its justification depends on other justified beliefs. Where some *b* is offered by a foundationalist as a basic belief, the reason for S's justification in thinking it true should be statable in the form of a principle of justification for basic beliefs. This argument has it that because such *b*s are justified by reference to the beliefs constituting the principle, they cannot therefore be basic, and anyway the principle would itself have to be known or justified if justified belief is to arise in accordance with it – which, for the same reasons as sketched, leads to regress.

This criticism is constructed from essentially similar variants levelled against foundationalism by Sellars, Lehrer and Bonjour among others.[5] Their intention is to show, by means of this argument, that foundationalism is implausible *ab initio.* I shall now show that foundationalism can be defended against it.

The antifoundationalist argument just sketched begs the very question of regress that foundationalism is devised to combat. It assumes that if any *b* is justified, it is so in virtue of antecedently justified beliefs, and cannot be justified in any other way. Thus it holds in effect that there can be no principles of justification for something which, on the basis of them, would be called 'basic'

[4] Cf. L. Bonjour, 'The coherence of empirical knowledge', *Philosophical Studies* 30 (1976), pp. 284-5 and J. Von Cleve, 'Foundationalism, epistemic principles, and the Cartesian circle', *Philosophical Review* 88 (1979), pp. 74ff. I am indebted to their highly interesting papers for some of the following points.

[5] Cf. Bonjour, op. cit., for an overview of these.

beliefs; for any putative principle of justification for beliefs which foundationalists wish to hold basic must itself consist in justifiable beliefs of the form: any *b* is justified in virtue of φ, and this *b* has φ. This is to say that the only form of justification principle there can be, on this anti-foundationalist view, is a *transmission* principle. And finally, the criticism holds that any such principle must itself be justified for S at *t* if it justifies any *b*, which is a further source of regress. On all counts the criticism fails.

This can be seen by noting that the general form of justification principles is not as characterised in the foregoing criticism, and that the general form allows a sharp distinction between transmission principles and principles for the justification of basic beliefs.[6] In general, a justification principle has the form 'if ... then *b* is justified for S'. In transmission principles, the blank is filled by epistemically evaluated propositions. In a principle for justification of basic beliefs, the antecedent will not contain epistemic evaluations, but instead a specification of some set of circumstances such that when these obtain, the basic belief mentioned in the consequent is justified in virtue of their obtaining. Thus – to take two examples at random – the circumstances may consist in something S is doing (for example perhaps 'clearly and distinctly' perceiving that something is the case, as Descartes might say) or some state that S is in (for example a 'self-presenting state', as Chisholm would say). This correction of the criticism's point about principles allows that, assuming a satisfactory statement of such a principle, not all beliefs must be justified solely in terms of antecedently justified beliefs, but could be justified in virtue of some such principle. In other words, it is not the case, as the antifoundationalist critique implies, that there cannot be principles of justification for foundational beliefs *in principle*; i.e. that nothing could count as such.

Nor is it the case that a principle for the justification of basic beliefs needs to be justified for S at *t* in order for him to be justified in believing some non-basic *b* at *t*, i.e. that S needs to know that the principle is true in order that the circumstances stated to obtain by its antecedent can justify his belief that *b*. For, the circumstances stated as obtaining in the antecedent are *sufficient* for S's being justified in

[6] Cf. van Cleve, op. cit., pp. 75-6, whose characterisation of the general form of justification principle is adopted here.

believing that *b*; and it is logically true that if *x* is sufficient for *y*, then there is no other condition *z* such that it is necessary for *y*, unless it is also necessary for *x*. It is not logically necessary for the obtaining of the circumstances stated to obtain in the principle's antecedent, that the principle be known. Therefore the principle does not have to be known in order for justified belief to arise in accordance with it (cf. van Cleve, ibid.). (It does not follow from this, of course, that a foundationalist is exempted from the task of giving a satisfactory account of the principles at issue!)

The refutation of the anti-foundationalist argument sketched above does not show that foundationalism is true; it shows only that it is not misguided or implausible *ab initio*, which is the claim antifoundationalists make in trying to show in a wholly general way that one cannot make appeal to a notion of basic beliefs. The success of any particular epistemological theory of justification which is foundationalist in character depends, as for any philosophical theory, on the merits of its detailed setting-out; the considerations dealt with here are far from being ones of detail.

For any theory which is foundationalist in character, the following features are therefore central. It must furnish a satisfactory account of basic beliefs, of the principles of justification for them, and of the principles governing the transmission of justification from basic beliefs through the corpus of beliefs based on them. There are no restrictions on any of these issues specifiable in advance of dealing with them in detail, save two; that the basic beliefs not be derivable from antecedently justified beliefs, but be somehow self-sufficient and able to bear the weight of the corpus of beliefs based upon them; and that any justified belief other than a basic belief be so justified ultimately by reference to these basic beliefs. In so far as the theory constructed in Chapter 2 satisfies these requirements, it is a foundationalist theory; in so far as it is a successful theory, it vindicates foundationalism.

APPENDIX 4

The forms of scepticism

It will be useful to note the general forms which sceptical arguments can take.[1] A sceptical thesis can be viewed as one relating to a class of propositions, in the present case a class of propositions constituting claims that matters are thus and such in the world. The claim made by the sceptic regarding the class of propositions in question is that each member of the class is doubtful in some manner and degree. Showing how doubt arises in connection with propositions of the given class involves the sceptic in furnishing considerations of sufficient plausibility to make out his case; which is to say that he has *some* positive work to do in supporting his thesis, although this can be minimal.

A sceptical thesis of this kind would of course be a local one in virtue of its being addressed to a given class of propositions about a given range of items. There can be universal scepticism too, which would be a thesis to the effect that no proposition whatever can be known or justifiably believed. Because a wholly universal thesis to this effect would exclude necessary statements along with all others, and therefore collaterally or directly impugns reason,[2] it has a high initial degree of implausibility owing to its own proscriptions falling upon the statements by which they are themselves expressed. It frequently happens that universal scepticism is in fact not quite universal, admitting necessary truths and sometimes first-person phenomenal statements, and it is usually attached to scepticism about *knowledge* in some stringently defined sense.[3]

Together with this distinction between local and universal

[1] The classifications to follow are based on those made by Pappas in a very helpful paper 'Focus on epistemological scepticism' in Pappas and Swain, *Essays on Knowledge and Justification*, London 1978, pp. 309-16.

[2] Hume and Unger afford examples: Hume, *Treatise* I iv. § 1. P. Unger, *Ignorance*, Oxford 1975, passim, esp. pp. 223ff.

[3] Cf. Pappas, op. cit., p. 312.

scepticism, it is useful to make another, this time between scepticism about knowledge as such (KS) and scepticism about justification (JS). KS is in general the view that no proposition (at all, if universal; or in a given class, if local) can be known to be true, or (a weaker version) is known to be true; JS is the view that no proposition (universally; or, in a class) can ever be justified for a person, or (weaker) is justified for a person. The different strengths which KS and JS can have range, as noted, from, for example, KS claims to the effect that it is logically impossible for all, or a class, of propositions to be known, to claims that as a matter of fact none in a class are known; and so *mutatis mutandis* for JS, although given that there are degrees of strength for justification itself, the number of forms scepticism might take is increased according as to whether it is scepticism about complete justification, or scepticism about there ever being a better than ·5 probability for the truth of some claims, or justification *tout court*.[4] In this way the number of possible variant forms which a sceptical thesis might take is high, even – in overview – bewilderingly so. This accounts for the variety of sceptical positions proferred in the literature, especially the contemporary literature, of epistemology (cf. Pappas, ibid), and it signals a danger; that one can all too readily construct a sceptical position just suited to one's project of defeating or defending it. This, as witness the work of, for example, Ryle and Austin, happens altogether too frequently.

That there can be a large number of possible variations in sceptical positions need not be troublesome. Certain considerations narrow the range to governable limits. These arise from adopting the tactic of looking at the degree of strength sceptical theses themselves have. It is clear that strong sceptical theses are in danger of being self-defeating: a thesis urging the logical impossibility of any justification for believing anything whatever makes the thesis itself incredible because self-refuting.[5] Or, its strength may make it vacuous; if it has it that nothing whatever can be known with utter certainty, then, because it does nothing to rule out our having powerfully justified beliefs (of which it might be one), it does no harm.

On the whole, KS and all universal forms of scepticism are likely

[4] Pappas cites the writers who have espoused one or other of the forms strong, weak, universal or local KS and JS.

[5] Unger accepts this but faults language rather than his own logic.

to have a high degree of implausibility themselves, so that whether or not they pose a serious challenge will depend upon how carefully they are formulated and what restrictions are placed upon them by their formulators. JS for a given class of propositions about the external world is much more sinister because much more plausible both in overview and in detail.

In the recent past there have been some quick dismissals of universal KS or other overly strong sceptical positions, from which, on the mistaken ground that these were *the* sceptical arguments, it was concluded that scepticism is bunk.[6] JS relative to a class of propositions remains, however, as a persistent and genuinely problematic scepticism, and it is this scepticism which, as it seems to me, has been at the root of serious attempts to construct satisfactory epistemological theories.[7] This is the scepticism with which I am concerned here.

APPENDIX 5

Realism and perceptual discourse

A point that Austin raises, and Ayer comments on, in connection with the intimate link between talk of the world and experience of the world is of great importance. Austin remarks in criticism of Ayer and Warnock that 'statements of "immediate perception", so far from being that from which we *advance* to more ordinary statements, are actually arrived at by *retreating from* more ordinary statements, by progressive hedging'.[1] Ayer responded by saying that this observation would be effective if in fact he and Warnock held the thesis that we accumulate experiential statements before venturing perceptual statements; but it fails because they are not claiming that a conscious process of this sort is gone through, but instead that perceptual statements are 'based upon (experiential statements) just in the sense that it is necessary for any perceptual statement to be

[6] Moore, Ryle and Austin spring to mind in this connection.
[7] Thus the work of, for example, Russell, Ayer and Chisholm.
[1] J.L. Austin, *Sense & Sensibilia*, Oxford 1961, p. 141.

true that some experiential statement be true, but possible for the experiential statement to be true even though the perceptual statement is false'.[2] Thus the experiential statements are primary in the sense that they constitute the logical grounds for, not psychological antecedents of, perceptual statements, which point is 'not in the least invalidated by the fact that their role is brought to light by ... the process of retreating from more ordinary statements'. And Ayer went on to say that with sufficient ingenuity and labour a purely sensory vocabulary could be constructed to describe experience without trading upon the vocabulary of physical objects. However, 'the fact would remain that the character of our experiences themselves is affected by our beliefs concerning the physical world, beliefs which are incorporated in the language which we first learn to speak', a point, says Ayer, not hitherto given due weight by sense-data theorists, but which does not affect their logical thesis.

Now, this is an important matter. Austin's observations and the later part of Ayer's reply legitimately prompt one to raise the crucial question whether an account of experience *can* be given which does not make essential reference to the external world as what (as we would pretheoretically say) the experience is experience 'of'. Ayer says it can; it is not clear whether Austin intended his observation to amount to a claim that *in principle* it cannot (i.e. rather than just as a matter of ordinary fact about which we need reminding, that it doesn't). However, Strawson explicitly urges this very point in discussing later views of Ayer's on the same head;[2] Strawson says, 'Whereas Ayer says we take a step beyond our sensible experience in making our perceptual judgments, I say rather that we take a step back (in general) from our perceptual judgments in framing accounts of our sensible experience; for we have (in general) to include a reference to the former in framing a veridical description of the latter.'[4] The reason for this, Strawson argues, is that in line with the Kantian notion that sensible experience presents itself as 'an *immediate* consciousness of the existence of things outside us' (p. 47), it seems unavoidable that we should view experience as permeated by

[2] A.J. Ayer, 'Has Austin refuted the sense-datum theory?', *Synthese* 1967.

[3] Ayer, *Central Questions*, chs. 4 and 5 passim.

[4] P.F. Strawson, 'Perception and its objects' in G.L. Macdonald (ed.), *Perception and Identity*, London 1979, pp. 45-6.

realist presumptions, and that the very character of that experience is determined by these presumptions in a way which makes them indispensable to a veridical characterisation of our experience itself. If this is right, then there cannot be a 'purely sensory vocabulary', because talk of experience must involve reference to its objects, taken, in an uncomplicated ontological sense of realism, realistically.

Ayer's recourse was to say that he is not claiming that we go through a process of inferring statements about physical objects from statements about experience, but that it is a matter of giving an account of our experience, because the reason we have 'to believe in the existence of physical objects (lies) in the character of our sense experience', and therefore even although our experience is 'permeated' by realist presumptions, and is originally organised in their favour, this does not entail that our sensible experience and the realist view we take are indistinguishable.[5] 'On the contrary, they need to be distinguished' (p. 293), because it is open that our 'primitive realist presumptions', as Strawson follows Mackie in calling them, can be called in question relative to some other theory about the course of our experience of the Lockean or scientific realist sort. (In fact Ayer takes Strawson to have allowed that our primitive presumptions *can* be called in question, although it is precisely Strawson's point that they cannot, for which reason Strawson holds that there can be no description of our experience in terms not involving what our realist presumptions make of them.)

Now, where the centre of the dispute between Ayer and his critics lies, it seems to me, is with the issue of what is to be regarded as *ultimately* important in founding or justifying our belief in the existence of physical objects. I think some reconciliatory manoeuvres can be made. Ayer throughout his work insists that sensory experience is the first and last court in connection with our belief in physical objects, which is why it is for him vital to get a proper characterisation of such experience independently of the ontological weight it carries, and the manner of whose bearing by experience it is crucial to show. Austin, and more explicitly Strawson, argue that sensory experience cannot be characterised independently of what we take it to be experience of; Strawson's reason is the strong one that concepts about the objective existence of what our experience is of

[5] Ayer in Macdonald, op. cit., pp. 289-93.

constitute the grounds of possibility for that experience itself. But the division of opinion is by no means as profound as it seems. Ayer grants a significant part of Strawson's (and Austin's) point about the role our beliefs play in having experiences; and, as it seems to me, his insistence on the need for an independent characterisation of experience can therefore be viewed as an anxiety he feels about the extent to which admitting this point endangers the equally valid point that the major source both of our beliefs about matters of fact and our checkings of our beliefs about matters of fact is, centrally, sensory experience. Such anxiety could be allayed by showing that Strawson, at any rate, is committed, and rightly so, to what he has called 'Kant's Principle of Significance', which is that 'there can be no legitimate, or even meaningful, employment of ideas or concepts which does not relate them to empirical or experiential conditions of their application' (*Bounds of Sense*, p. 16). Understanding this in the strong sense intended by Strawson, that is, that one must be able to *specify* the kind of experience-situation in which a concept is to be applied if it is to be legitimately applied, reserves to experience a crucial and central role in our epistemology. This accords with Ayer's chief point; what is then required is acceptance of the fact that experience's role is not *exclusive*, and that the full story is told only when the experience-organising concepts, along the line of the role assigned to them in Kant's insight, are allowed equal status at the foundation. As I argue in the main body of the book, these two issues must be taken together for the full story to be told; and an important part of what this claim amounts to is that reference to objectivity concepts *is* indeed essential to the characterisation of experience.

APPENDIX 6

A note on certainty

Quinton usefully distinguishes, in all, five uses of 'certain' in philosophical discussion.[1] In one, 'certain' is construed as 'psychologically indubitable', in the sense that *S* is subjectively convinced that *p*. A second construal has 'certain' as 'logically necessary', a very stringent notion because it imputes to contingent propositions *inherent* doubtfulness. A third construal is of 'certain' as what Quinton calls 'self-authenticating', that is, propositions whose truth is guaranteed by the manner in which they are expressed – the *cogito* is a chief example. The fourth and fifth are the senses most frequently found discussed; 'certain' as 'incorrigible' and as 'beyond reasonable doubt'. Quinton in his discussion of incorrigibility also distinguishes 'incorrigible' statements from a closely related kind, namely 'self-intimating' statements. A statement is infallible or incorrigible, 'if its truth follows from the fact that it is believed ... (it) is one which is wholly verified by the experience that prompts its assertion, whose claim coincides with the evidence on which it is based. It has no predictive consequences whose failure to occur might refute it' (p. 147). The contrast is that if 'I am in pain' is incorrigible, it is possible both that I can be in pain and not believe 'that I am in pain'; what is ruled out is that when I am in pain I should believe 'that I am not in pain'. But the possibility that I should be in pain yet not believe that I am is ruled out (together with its denial) if 'I am in pain' is self-intimating; on this construal, if I am in pain I must know (and therefore believe) that I am (ibid.). Finally, there is the weaker notion of 'certain' as 'beyond reasonable doubt', which construal Quinton associates with Moore chiefly, Austin, and – incorrectly – Wittgenstein (p. 148). What is wrong with saying that Wittgenstein followed Moore in viewing 'certain' like this is that it seems to be precisely Wittgenstein's thought, prompted by but going

[1] A.M. Quinton, *The Nature of Things*, London 1975, pp. 144-9.

beyond Moore, that doubt and certainty arise only in situations where it is the case regarding some *p* that (a) in order to assert *p* one must have evidence for it and (b) it is possible to be mistaken in taking that evidence to be a ground for asserting *p*.[2] The propositions offered by Moore as ones of which he was certain – 'This is a hand' – are not, according to Wittgenstein, propositions of this kind; they play a 'logical role' in the language, such that it makes no sense to doubt them, and therefore no sense to claim to know them, because they are not propositions which are backed by evidence (to which having evidence is appropriate or relevant): accordingly, because it makes no sense to doubt them, it *also* makes no sense to say that one knows them (ibid. 250, 245 and 504). So a proposition about which we feel certain is for Wittgenstein not one which is 'beyond reasonable doubt', but one which it does not make sense (= infects the grounds of sense of the language) to doubt. (In any case, certainty is a psychological state for Wittgenstein, not a property of units of the language;[3] but one can paraphrase away the difficulty this entails). In the main body of this book, the sense in which transcendental beliefs are beyond question is the sense Wittgenstein gives to this notion. All the other senses of 'certain' identified by Quinton capture something of this notion except for the weak 'beyond reasonable doubt' construal, which for philosophical purposes is nigh useless since it concedes too much to scepticism.

[2] L. Wittgenstein, *On Certainty*, Oxford 1977, 243; cf. 483, 550.
[3] N. Malcolm, *Knowledge and Certainty*, Englewood Cliffs 1965, pp. 87-8.

Bibliography

Austin, J.L., *Sense and Sensibilia*, Oxford 1961

Ayer, A.J., *The Concept of a Person*, London 1963

'Has Austin refuted the sense-datum theory?' *Synthese* 67 (1967)

The Central Questions of Philosophy, London 1973

Bishop, J., 'More thought on thought and talk', *Mind* 89 (1980)

Bennett, J., *Kant's Analytic*, London 1966

Berriman, W.A., 'Strawson's *Individuals* as descriptive metaphysics', *Australian Journal of Philosophy* 45 (1967)

Black, M., *Language and Philosophy*, Ithaca 1949

Bonjour, L., 'The coherence of empirical knowledge', *Philosophical Studies* 88 (1979)

Carnap, R., 'Empiricism, semantics and ontology' in *Meaning and Necessity*, Chicago 1956

Cornman, J.W., *Materialism and Sensations*, New York 1971

Davidson, D., 'Reality without reference', *Dialectica* 31 (1971)

'On the very idea of a conceptual scheme', *Proceedings of the American Philosophical Association* (1974)

'The method of truth in metaphysics' in French et al. 1979

Donnellan, K.S., 'Reference and definite descriptions' in Schwarz 1977

Dummett, M.A.E., 'What is a theory of meaning? I' in S. Guttenplan 1975

'What is a theory of meaning? II' in Evans & McDowell 1976

'The significance of Quine's indeterminacy thesis' in *Truth and Other Enigmas*, London 1979

Evans, G. & McDowell, J. (edd.), *Truth and Meaning*, Oxford 1976

Feyerband, P., *Against Method*, London 1978

Fogelin, R.J., *Evidence and Meaning*, London 1967

French, P.A., Uehling, T.E. & Wettstein, H.K. (edd.), *Contemporary Perspectives in the Philosophy of Language*, Minneapolis 1979

Geach, P., *Mental Acts*, London 1957

Gettier, E., 'Is justified true belief knowledge?', *Analysis* 23 (1963)
Goodman, N., *Fact, Fiction and Forecast*, London 1954
Grayling, A.C., *An Introduction to Philosophical Logic*, Hassocks 1982
Guttenplan, S. (ed.), *Mind and Language*, New York 1975
Harrison, B.J., *Introduction to Philosophy of Language*, London 1979
Harrison, R., 'Strawson and outer objects', *Philosophical Quarterly* 20 (1970)
On What There Must Be, Oxford 1974
Hintikka, J., 'Transcendental arguments genuine and spurious', *Nous* 61 (1972)
Hinton, J.M., *Experiences*, Oxford 1973
Hobbs, A., 'New phenomenalism as an account of perceptual knowledge' in Vesey 1976
Korner, S., 'The impossibility of transcendental deduction', *Monist* 51 (1967)
Kuhn, T., *The Structure of Scientific Revolutions*, Chicago 1962
Lehrer, K., *Knowledge*, Oxford 1974
Macdonald, G.L. (ed.), *Perception and Identity*, London 1979
McGinn, M., 'The third dogma of empiricism', *Proceedings of the Aristotelian Society* (1982) 1981-82
Mackie, J.L., *The Cement of the Universe*, Oxford 1974
Problems from Locke, Oxford 1976
'What's really wrong with phenomenalism?' *Proceedings of the British Academy* 55 (1968)
Malcolm, N., *Knowledge and Certainty*, Englewood Cliffs 1965
Pappas, G.S., 'Focus on epistemological scepticism' in Pappas & Swain
Pappas, G.S. & Swain, M. (edd.), *Essays on Knowledge and Justification*, New York 1978
Phillips, C., 'Constructivism and epistemology', *Philosophy* 53 (1978)
Phillips Griffiths, A. & Macintosh, J.J., 'Transcendental arguments' (Symposium), *Proceedings of the Aristotelian Society* supp. 43 (1969)
Putnam, H., *Meaning and the Moral Sciences*, London 1978
Quine, W.V.O., *Word and Object*, Cambridge, Mass. 1960
Theories and Things, Cambridge, Mass. 1981
Ontological Relativity and Other Essays, New York 1961
Quinton, A.M., *The Nature of Things*, London 1975
Rosenberg, J., 'Transcendental arguments revisited', *Journal of Philosophy* 25 (1975)

'Reply to Stroud', *Philosophical Studies* 31 (1977)
Russell, B., *Human Knowledge: Its Scope and Limits*, London 1948
Mysticism and Logic, London 1956
Ryle, G., *Dilemmas*, Cambridge 1954
Sainsbury, R.M.S., *Russell*, London 1979
Schaper, E., 'Arguing transcendentally', *Kant-Studien* 63 (1972)
Schwartz, S.P. (ed.), *Naming, Necessity and Natural Kinds*, New York 1977
Scruton, R., 'Objectivity and will', *Mind* 82 (1973)
Smith, G.W., 'The concepts of a sceptic', *Philosophy* 49 (1974)
Strawson, P., *Logico-Linguist Papers*, London 1971
The Bounds of Sense, London 1966
Individuals, London 1959
'Perception and its objects' in Macdonald 1979
Stroud, B., 'Transcendental arguments', *Journal of Philosophy* 65 (1968)
'Transcendental arguments and "epistemological naturalism" ', *Philosophical Studies* 31 (1971)
Transcendental Arguments and Science, Dordrecht 1979
Unger, P., *Ignorance*, Oxford 1975
Vesey, G., *Impressions of Empiricism*, London 1976
Von Cleve, J., 'Foundationalism, epistemic principles and the Cartesian circle', *Philosophical Review* 88 (1979)
Walker, R.C.S., *Kant*, London 1979
Ward, K., 'The ascription of experience', *Mind* 79 (1970)
Wilkerson, T.E., 'Transcendental arguments', *Philosophical Quarterly* 20 (1970)
Kant's Critique of Pure Reason, London 1976
Williams, M., *Groundless Belief*, London 1977
Wittgenstein, L., *Philosophical Investigations*, Oxford 1952
On Certainty, Oxford 1969

Index

antirealism, 13, 25-32, 46-7, 95, 110-13
Aristotle, 86
assertibility, *see* Warranted assertibility
Austin, J.L., i, 15, 81, 139, Appendix 5, 144
Ayer, A.J., i, ii, 14, 17-19, 97n, 125-7, Appendix 5

belief, Appendix 2 *passim*
Bennett, J., 78
Berkeley, G., 87, 111, 134
Berriman, W.A., 79n
Bishop, J., 52
Black, M., 56
Bonjour, L., 135

Carnap, R., 41-9, 66n, 75
certainty, Appendix 6
Chisholm, R., 136, 140n
conceptual scheme, 2, 3, 10, Chapter 3 *passim*, 77, 89-90, 116
Cornman, J.W., 133n
criteria, 28-30, 134

Davidson, D., 49-76, 189
Descartes, R., i, 15n, 90, 130, 134
Donnellan, K.S., 36
Dummett, M.A.E., 20, 25-7, 31n, 70n, 71

empiricism, 6-20, 74-5, 114, 122-5
Evans, G., 26n
experience, 3, Chapter 2 *passim*, Appendix 1

Feigl, H., 14
Feyerabend, P., 57-9, 62
Fogelin, R.J., 30n
foundationalism, 4, 8, 109-10, 114, Appendix 3
French, P.A., 67n

Geach, P., 51n
general beliefs, 10-14, 21
Gettier, E., 128
Giaquinto, M., ii
Goodman, N., 121n
Grayling, A.C., 112n, 114n
Guttenplan, S., 27n

Hamlyn, D.W., ii
Harrison, B.J., 69
Harrison, R., 81, 82, 115
Hintikka, J., 79-83
Hinton, J.M., 19
Hobbs, A., 20n
Hume, D., i, 7-9, 77, 87, 91, 111, 116, 118-20, 127, 138n

idealism, 34-35, 86-87, 92
internal-external distinction, *see* Carnap

justification, 1, 5, 38-9, Appendix 2, Appendix 3, 137-9

Kant, I, i, 4, 14, 17,. 35, 48, 76, 78-83, 85, 88, 91, 92-3, 101-2, 103, 111, 114-16, 122, 125, 127, 141, 143
knowledge, 1, Appendix 2 *passim*, 138
Korner, S., 54, 83, 89, 106

Kripke, S., 12-13
Kuhn, T., 61-2, 75

Lear, J., ii
Lehrer, K., 133n, 135
Leibniz, G., 117, 118
Locke, J., 116-18, 124, 125, 127
logical possibility, 27-8
Luntley, M., ii

MacDonald, G., 141n, 142n
Mackie, J., 50, 75, 83, 87, 89, 90, 106, 116-18, 127, 142
Malcolm, N., 144n
McDowell, J., 26n
McGinn, M., 60n
McNaughton, D., ii
Mill, J.S., 23
Moore, G.E., 140n, 144

naturalism, 7-9, Chapter 2 *passim*, 77, 91
Newton, I., 118

objects, 3, 15-39, 41-3, 45-8, 111-12

Pappas, G.S., 137-9
Peirce, C.S., 11
perception and perceptual beliefs, Chapter 2 *passim*, 110-13, Appendix 1
phenomenalism, 16-20
Phillips, C., 28-9
psychologism, 31, 124-5
Putnam, H., 86

Quine, W.V.O., 31, 49, 55, 56-7, 60n, 68-9, 70-1, 73, 74
Quinton, A., ii, 25, 43, 143-5

realism, 25-8, 47-8, 92, 98, 110-13, 116
reference, 22
relativism, 13, Chapter 3 *passim*
Rosenberg, J., 79n
rules, 8
Russell, B., 116, 120-2
Ryle, G., 23-4, 82, 139

Sainsbury, R.M.S., 121
scepticism, 1-9, 27-8, 40-1, 91-3, 97-109, Appendix 2, 132, Appendix 4 *passim*
Schaper, E., 79n
Schwartz, S.P., 36n
Scruton, R., 44n
Sellars, W., 135
sense, *see* Warranted assertibility
sense-data, 15, 16-20
Smith, G.W., 97n
Sprigge, T.L.S., ii
Strawson, P., ii, 7n, 12, 13n, 15, 17, 44-5, 49, 61-2, 78n, 79, 81, 82, 85, 88, 94, 97-109, 115, 141-3
Stroud, B., ii, 43, 78-9n, 88, 98-109, 112-13, 119

theory of error, 2, 21-39
transcendental argument, 2-4, 18, Chapter 4 *passim*, 127
transcendental beliefs, 2-3, 4-5, 10, 13, Chapter 2 *passim*, 114, 127
translation, *see* Relativism
truth, 12, 23-4, 37-9

Unger, P., 86, 138n, 139n

verification and verificationism, 13, 26-7, 28, 105-9, 112-13
Von Cleve, J., 135n, 136n, 137

Walker, R.C.S., 4n, 79n
Ward, K., 97n
Warnock, G., 140
warrant and warranted assertibility, 20-39, 97
Wilkerson, T.E., 94
Williams, M., 129, 133n
Wittgenstein, L., i, 7-9, 28, 52, 77, 81, 91, 99, 144